new interchange

English for international communication

Jack C. Richards

with Jonathan Hull and Susan Proctor

student's

book

2

New Interchange Student's Book
revision prepared by Jack C. Richards.

CAMBRIDGE
UNIVERSITY PRESS

PUBLISHED BY THE PRESS SYNDICATE OF THE UNIVERSITY OF CAMBRIDGE
The Pitt Building, Trumpington Street, Cambridge CB2 1RP, United Kingdom

CAMBRIDGE UNIVERSITY PRESS
The Edinburgh Building, Cambridge CB2 2RU, United Kingdom
40 West 20th Street, New York, NY 10011-4211, USA
10 Stamford Road, Oakleigh, Melbourne 3166, Australia

First published 1997
Second printing 1998
New Interchange Student's Book 2 has been developed from *Interchange* Student's Book 2,
first published by Cambridge University Press in 1991.

Printed in the United States of America
Typeset in New Century Schoolbook

Library of Congress Cataloging-in-Publication Data
Richards, Jack C.
New interchange: English for international communication :
student's book 2 / Jack C. Richards with Jonathan Hull and Susan
Proctor.
p. cm.
Rev. ed. of: Interchange : English for international communication :
student's book 2. 1991.
ISBN 0-521-62862-8
1. English language – Textbooks for foreign speakers.
2. Communication, International – Problems, exercises, etc.
I. Hull, Jonathan. II. Proctor, Susan. III. Richards,
Jack C. Interchange. IV. Title.
PE1128.R4593   1997
428.2'4 – dc21   97-27440
                                                        CIP

A catalogue record for this book is available from the British Library.

ISBN 0 521 62862 8 Student's Book 2   ISBN 0 521 62849 0 Video 2 (NTSC)
ISBN 0 521 62861 X Student's Book 2A   ISBN 0 521 62848 2 Video 2 (PAL)
ISBN 0 521 62860 1 Student's Book 2B   ISBN 0 521 62847 4 Video 2 (SECAM)
ISBN 0 521 62859 8 Workbook 2   ISBN 0 521 62846 6 Video Activity Book 2
ISBN 0 521 62858 X Workbook 2A   ISBN 0 521 62845 8 Video Teacher's Guide 2
ISBN 0 521 62857 1 Workbook 2B
ISBN 0 521 62856 3 Teacher's Edition 2   *Available from the First Edition*
ISBN 0 521 62855 5 Teacher's Manual 2   ISBN 0 521 46759 4 Placement Test
ISBN 0 521 62854 7 Class Audio Cassettes 2   ISBN 0 521 42219 1 Lab Cassette Set 2
ISBN 0 521 62852 0 Student's Audio Cassette 2A   ISBN 0 521 42220 5 Lab Guide 2
ISBN 0 521 62652 8 Student's Audio Cassette 2B
ISBN 0 521 62853 9 Class Audio CDs 2   *Available in mid-1998*
ISBN 0 521 62851 2 Student's Audio CD 2A   ISBN 0 521 62882 2 Placement Test (revised)
ISBN 0 521 62850 4 Student's Audio CD 2B

Book design, art direction, and layout services: Adventure House, NYC
Illustrators: Adventure House, Jack and Judith DeGaffenreid, Susann Ferris Jones, Randy Jones, Mark Kaufman,
Kevin Spaulding, Bill Thomson, Sam Viviano
Photo researcher: Sylvia P. Bloch

Introduction

THE NEW EDITION

New Interchange is a revision of *Interchange*, one of the world's most successful and popular English courses. *New Interchange* incorporates many improvements suggested by teachers and students from around the world. Some major changes include many new Conversations, Snapshots, and Readings; more extensive Grammar Focus models and activities; a greater variety and amount of listening materials; extensive changes to the **Teacher's Edition** and **Workbook**; and additions to the **Video.**

New Interchange is a multi-level course in English as a second or foreign language for young adults and adults. The course covers the four skills of listening, speaking, reading, and writing, as well as improving pronunciation and building vocabulary. Particular emphasis is placed on listening and speaking. The primary goal of the course is to teach communicative competence, that is, the ability to communicate in English according to the situation, purpose, and roles of the participants. The language used in *New Interchange* is American English; however, the course reflects the fact that English is the major language of international communication and is not limited to any one country, region, or culture. Level Two is for intermediate students and takes them from the low-intermediate up to the intermediate level.

Level Two builds on the foundations for accurate and fluent communication already established in *Intro* and Level One by extending grammatical, lexical, and functional skills. The syllabus covered here in Level Two also incorporates a review of key language features from Level One, allowing Student's Book 2 to be used with students who have not studied with Level One.

COURSE LENGTH

Each full level of *New Interchange* contains between 70 and 120 hours of class instruction time. For classes where more time is available, the Teacher's Edition gives detailed suggestions for Optional Activities to extend each unit. Where less time is available, the amount of time spent on Interchange Activities, Reading, Writing, Optional Activities, and the Workbook can be reduced.

Each split edition contains approximately 35 to 60 hours of classroom material. The Student's Book, Workbook, and Student's Audio Cassettes or CDs are available in split editions.

COURSE COMPONENTS

The **Student's Book** contains 16 six-page units. The exercises in each unit are grouped into two topical and/or functional sections; these sections are referred to as "cycles" in the teaching notes. There are four review units. There are a set of communication tasks called Interchange Activities and Unit Summaries at the back of the book.

The full-color **Teacher's Edition** features page-by-page instructions interleaved with reproductions of the Student's Book pages. The instructions contain detailed suggestions on how to teach the course, lesson-by-lesson notes, numerous follow-up suggestions for optional tasks and Optional Activities, complete answer keys, and transcripts of the listening activities. Located at the back of the book are instructions for the Interchange Activities, an Optional Activities Index and Additional Optional Activities, answers to Workbook exercises, four photocopiable achievement tests for use in class, transcripts for the tests, and test answer keys. A noninterleaved, black-and-white **Teacher's Manual** is also available.

The **Workbook** provides a variety of exercises that develop students' proficiency with the grammar, reading, writing, spelling, and vocabulary presented in the Student's Book. Each six-page unit follows the same teaching sequence as the Student's Book. Most Workbook units also contain "review exercises" that recycle teaching points from previous units in the context of the new topic. The Workbook can be used for classwork or for homework.

The **Class Audio Cassettes** or **CDs** are for use in the classroom. They contain natural-sounding recordings of the Conversations, Grammar Focus models, Pronunciation exercises, and Listening activities in the Student's Book, and the listening exercises for the tests. A variety of native-speaker voices and accents, as well as some nonnative speakers of English, are used. Exercises that are recorded are indicated with the symbol.

The **Student's Audio Cassettes** or **CDs** are for self-study by students. They contain recordings of the Conversations, Pronunciation exercises, and Grammar Focus models from the Student's Book. They are available in split editions only.

The **Video** is designed to review and extend the topics and language presented in the Student's Book. It contains sixteen entertaining, dramatized sequences based on the language and vocabulary in the Student's Book. There are also five authentic documentary sequences. The accompanying **Video Activity Book** provides comprehension and conversation activities, as well as language practice. The **Video Teacher's Guide** provides thorough instructional support, a complete answer key, and photocopiable transcripts of the video sequences.

The **CD-ROM** (available in Mac and PC formats) is intended to be used in conjunction with the Student's Book to review and practice the language learned in class. The CD-ROM can be used on a home computer or in a language laboratory. At the core of each of the sixteen units is a video sequence taken from the *New Interchange* Video, and some of the activities are based on ones found in the Video Activity Book. In total, the CD-ROM contains over 150 activities; students do the activities they want to do at the touch of a button. In addition, there are four tests to check students' progress.

The **Placement Test** helps teachers and program administrators place their students at the most appropriate level of *New Interchange*. The booklet contains the listening, reading, and grammar sections on photocopiable pages, and instructions for administering the oral placement exam. The listening section is accompanied by a cassette.

The set of four **Lab Cassettes** and the accompanying **Lab Guide** from the first edition of *Interchange* can be used in conjunction with the *New Interchange* series.

APPROACH AND METHODOLOGY

New Interchange teaches students to use English for everyday situations and purposes related to school, social life, work, and leisure. The underlying philosophy is that learning a second or foreign language is more rewarding, meaningful, and effective when the language is used for authentic communication. Throughout *New Interchange*, students are presented with natural and useful language. In addition, students have the opportunity to personalize the language they learn, make use of their own knowledge and experiences, and express their ideas and opinions.

KEY FEATURES

Adult and International Content *New Interchange* deals with contemporary topics that are of high interest and relevant to both students and teachers. The topics have been selected for their interest to both homogenous and heterogenous classes.

Integrated Syllabus *New Interchange* has an integrated, multi-skills syllabus that links topics, communicative functions, and grammar. Grammar – seen as an essential component of second and foreign language proficiency and competence – is always presented communicatively, with controlled accuracy-based activities leading to fluency-based communicative practice. In this way, there is a link between grammatical form and communicative function. The syllabus is carefully graded, with a gradual progression of teaching items.

Enjoyable and Useful Learning Activities A variety of interesting and enjoyable activities provides thorough individual student practice and enables learners to apply the language they learn. The course also makes extensive use of information-gap tasks; role plays; and pair, group, and whole class activities. Task-based and information-sharing activities provide a maximum amount of student-generated communication.

WHAT EACH UNIT CONTAINS

Snapshot The Snapshots graphically present interesting real-world information that introduces the topic of a unit or cycle, and also develop vocabulary. Follow-up questions encourage discussion of the Snapshot material and personalize the topic.

Conversation The Conversations introduce the new grammar of each cycle in a communicative context and present functional and conversational expressions.

Grammar Focus The new grammar of each unit is presented in color boxes and is followed by controlled and freer communicative practice activities. These freer activities often have students use the grammar in a personal context.

Fluency Exercise These pair, group, whole class, or role-play activities provide more personal practice of the new teaching points and increase the opportunity for individual student practice.

Pronunciation These exercises focus on important features of spoken English, including stress, rhythm, intonation, reductions, and blending.

Listening The Listening activities develop a wide variety of listening skills, including listening for gist, listening for details, and inferring meaning from context. Charts or graphics often accompany these task-based exercises to lend support to students.

Word Power The Word Power activities develop students' vocabulary through a variety of interesting tasks, such as word maps and collocation exercises. Word Power activities are usually followed by oral or written practice that helps students understand how to use the vocabulary in context.

Writing The Writing exercises include practical writing tasks that extend and reinforce the teaching points in the unit and help develop student's compositional skills. The Teacher's Edition demonstrates how to use the models and exercises to focus on the process of writing.

Reading The reading passages use various types of texts adapted from authentic sources. The Readings develop a variety of reading skills, including reading for details, skimming, scanning, and making inferences. Also included are pre-reading and post-reading questions that use the topic of the reading as a springboard to discussion.

Interchange Activities The Interchange Activities are pair work, group work, or whole class activities involving information sharing and role playing to encourage real communication. These exercises are a central part of the course and allow students to extend and personalize what they have practiced and learned in each unit.

Unit Summaries Unit Summaries are located at the back of the Student's Book. They contain lists of the key vocabulary and functional expressions, as well as grammar extensions for each unit.

FROM THE AUTHORS

We hope that you will like using *New Interchange* and find it useful, interesting, and fun. Our goal has been to provide teachers and students with activities that make the English class a time to look forward to and, at the same time, provide students with the skills they need to use English outside the classroom. Please let us know how you enjoy it and good luck!

Jack C. Richards
Jonathan Hull
Susan Proctor

Authors' Acknowledgments

A great number of people contributed to the development of *New Interchange*. Particular thanks are owed to the following:

The **reviewers** using the first edition of *Interchange* in the following schools and institutes – the insights and suggestions of these teachers and their students have helped define the content and format of the new edition: Jorge Haber Resque, **Centro Cultural Brasil-Estados Unidos (CCBEU),** Belém, Brazil; Lynne Roecklein, **Gifu University,** Japan; Mary Oliveira and Montserrat M. Djmal, **Instituto Brasil-Estados Unidos (IBEU),** Rio de Janeiro, Brazil; Liliana Baltra, **Instituto Chileno Norte-Americano,** Santiago de Chile; Blanca Arazi and the teachers at **Instituto Cultural Argentino Norteamericano (ICANA),** Buenos Aires, Argentina; Mike Millin and Kelley Seymour, **James English School,** Japan; Matilde Legorreta and Manuel Hidalgo, **Kratos, S.A. de C.V.,** Mexico D.F.; Peg Donner, Ricia Doren, and Andrew Sachar, **Rancho Santiago College Centennial Education Center,** Santa Ana, California, USA; James Hale, **Sundai ELS,** Japan; Christopher Lynch, **Sunshine College,** Tokyo, Japan; Valerie Benson, **Suzugamine Women's**

College, Hiroshima, Japan; Michael Barnes, **Tokyu Be Seminar,** Japan; Claude Arnaud and Paul Chris McVay, **Toyo Women's College,** Tokyo, Japan; Maria Emilia Rey Silva, **UCBEU,** São Paulo, Brazil; Lilia Ortega Sepulveda, **Unidad Lomoa Hermosa,** Mexico D.F.; Eric Bray, **Kyoto YMCA English School,** Kyoto, Japan; John Pak, **Yokohama YMCA English School,** Yokohama, Japan; and the many teachers around the world who responded to the *Interchange* questionnaire.

The **editorial** and **production** team: Suzette André, Sylvia P. Bloch, John Borrelli, Mary Carson, Karen Davy, Samuela Eckstut, Randee Falk, Andrew Gitzy, Christa Hansen, Pauline Ireland, Stephanie Karras, Penny Laporte, Kathy Niemczyk, Kathleen Schultz, Rosie Stamp, and Mary Vaughn.

And Cambridge University Press **staff** and **advisors**: Carlos Barbisan, Kathleen Corley, Kate Cory-Wright, Riitta da Costa, Peter Davison, Peter Donovan, Robert Gallo, Cecilia Gómez, Colin Hayes, Thares Keeree, Jinsook Kim, Koen Van Landeghem, Alex Martinez, Carine Mitchell, Chuanpit Phalavadhana, Sabina Sahni, Helen Sandiford, Dan Schulte, Ian Sutherland, Chris White, Janaka Williams, and Ellen Zlotnick.

Plan of Book 2

Title/Topics	Functions	Grammar
UNIT 1 — PAGES 2–7		
A time to remember People; childhood; reminiscences	Introducing yourself; talking about yourself; exchanging personal information; remembering your childhood; asking about someone's childhood	Past tense; *used to* for habitual actions
UNIT 2 — PAGES 8–13		
Caught in the rush Transportation; transportation problems; city services	Talking about transportation and transportation problems; evaluating city services; asking for and giving information	Adverbs of quantity with countable and uncountable nouns: *too many, too much, not enough, more, fewer, less*; indirect questions from *Wh*-questions
UNIT 3 — PAGES 14–19		
Time for a change! Houses and apartments; lifestyle changes; wishes	Describing positive and negative features; making comparisons; talking about lifestyle changes; expressing wishes	Evaluations and comparisons with adjectives: *not . . . enough, too, not as . . . as, as . . . as*; Evaluations and comparisons with nouns: *not enough . . . , as many . . . as*; Wish
UNIT 4 — PAGES 20–25		
I've never heard of that! Food; recipes; instructions; cooking methods	Talking about food; expressing likes and dislikes; describing a favorite snack; giving instructions	Simple past vs. present perfect; sequence adverbs: *first, then, next, after that, finally*
REVIEW OF UNITS 1–4 — PAGES 26–27		
UNIT 5 — PAGES 28–33		
Going places Travel; vacations; plans	Describing vacation plans; giving travel advice; planning a vacation	Future with *be going to* and *will*; modals for necessity and suggestion: *(don't) have to, must, need to, better, ought to, should*
UNIT 6 — PAGES 34–39		
Sure. No problem! Complaints; household chores; requests; excuses; apologies	Making requests; accepting and refusing requests; complaining; apologizing; giving excuses	Two-part verbs; *will* for responding to requests; requests with modals and *Would you mind . . . ?*
UNIT 7 — PAGES 40–45		
What's this for? Technology; instructions	Describing technology; giving instructions; giving advice	Infinitives and gerunds; infinitive complements
UNIT 8 — PAGES 46–51		
Let's celebrate! Holidays; festivals; customs; celebrations	Describing holidays, festivals, customs, and special events	Relative clauses of time; adverbial clauses of time: *before, when, after*
REVIEW OF UNITS 5–8 — PAGES 52–53		

Title/Topics	Functions	Grammar
UNIT 9 PAGES 54–59		
Back to the future Life in the past, present, and future; changes and contrasts; consequences	Talking about change; comparing time periods; describing possibilities	Time contrasts; conditional sentences with *if* clauses
UNIT 10 PAGES 60–65		
I don't like working on weekends! Abilities and skills; job preferences; personality traits; careers	Describing abilities and skills; talking about job preferences; describing personality traits	Gerunds; short responses; clauses with *because*
UNIT 11 PAGES 66–71		
It's really worth seeing! Landmarks and monuments; aspects of countries; world knowledge	Talking about landmarks and monuments; describing countries; discussing facts	Passive with *by* (simple past); passive without *by* (simple present)
UNIT 12 PAGES 72–77		
It's been a long time! Information about someone's past; recent past events	Asking about someone's past; describing recent experiences	Past continuous vs. simple past; present perfect continuous
REVIEW OF UNITS 9–12 PAGES 78–79		
UNIT 13 PAGES 80–85		
A terrific book, but a terrible movie! Entertainment; movies and books; reactions and opinions	Describing movies and books; talking about actors and actresses; asking for and giving reactions and opinions	Participles as adjectives; relative clauses
UNIT 14 PAGES 86–91		
So that's what it means! Nonverbal communication; gestures and meanings; emotions; proverbs; signs and meanings; drawing conclusions	Interpreting body language; explaining gestures and meanings; describing emotions; explaining proverbs; asking about signs and meanings	Modals and adverbs: *might, may, could, must, maybe, perhaps, probably*; permission, obligation, and prohibition
UNIT 15 PAGES 92–97		
What would you do? Money; hopes; predicaments; speculations	Speculating about past and future events; describing a predicament; giving advice and suggestions	Unreal conditional sentences with *if* clauses; past modals
UNIT 16 PAGES 98–103		
What's your excuse? Requests; excuses; invitations; "white lies"	Reporting what people say; making requests; making invitations and excuses	Reported speech: requests; reported speech
REVIEW OF UNITS 13–16 PAGES 104–105		
UNIT SUMMARIES PAGES S2–S17		
APPENDIX		

Listening/Pronunciation	Writing/Reading	Interchange Activity
Listening to people talk about changes; listening to possible solutions to a problem Pitch	Writing about future hopes "Are You in Love?": Reading about the signs of being in love	"Consider the consequences": Agreeing and disagreeing with classmates
Listening for job requirements; listening to people talk about their interests; listening to personality traits Final *t* in *not*, *don't*, and *can't*	Writing a personality description "Find the job that's right for you!": Reading about how to find the perfect job	"Dream job": Hiring an employee
Listening to descriptions of monuments; listening for information about a country Linked sounds	Writing about a country "Seven Modern Wonders of the World": Reading about the modern wonders of the world	"Traveler's profile": Finding out about classmates' travel habits
Listening to people talk about events in their careers; listening for information about someone's recent past Contrastive stress	Writing a biography "Child Prodigies": Reading about child prodigies	"Life is like a game!": Finding out about classmates' lives
Listening for opinions; listening to a movie review Word and sentence stress	Writing a movie review "Star Wars": Reading three movie reviews	"At the movies": Asking classmates' opinions about movies and actors
Listening to people interpret meanings; listening to people talk about the meanings of signs Emphatic stress	Writing an interpretation of a proverb "Body Language: What Does It Say?": Reading about body language	"What's going on?": Interpreting body language
Listening to people talk about predicaments; listening to advice and suggestions Reduced form of *have*	Writing a letter asking for advice "Ask Alice": Reading an advice column	"Do the right thing!": Deciding what to do in a difficult situation
Listening for excuses; receiving telephone messages Reduced forms of *had*, *would*, and *was*	Writing telephone messages "The Truth About Lying": Reading about "white lies"	"Excuses, excuses": Making up excuses

A time to remember

1 SNAPSHOT

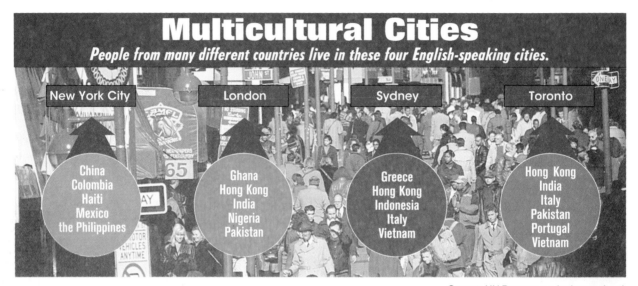

Multicultural Cities
People from many different countries live in these four English-speaking cities.

New York City	London	Sydney	Toronto
China Colombia Haiti Mexico the Philippines	Ghana Hong Kong India Nigeria Pakistan	Greece Hong Kong Indonesia Italy Vietnam	Hong Kong India Italy Pakistan Portugal Vietnam

Source: UN Department for International, Economic, and Social Affairs

Talk about these questions.

Why do you think these cities have so many immigrants?
Are there any immigrants in your city? Where are they from originally?

2 CONVERSATION

A Listen and practice.

Ted: Oh, I'm really sorry. Are you OK?
Ana: I'm fine. But I'm not very good at this.
Ted: Neither am I. Say, are you from South America?
Ana: Yes, I am, originally. I was born in Argentina.
Ted: Did you grow up there?
Ana: Yes, I did, but my family moved here
    eight years ago, when I was in high school.
Ted: And where did you learn to Rollerblade?
Ana: Here in the park. This is only my second time.
Ted: Well, it's my *first* time. Can you give me
    some lessons?
Ana: Sure. Just follow me.
Ted: By the way, my name is Ted.
Ana: And I'm Ana. Nice to meet you.

B Listen to the rest of the conversation.
What are two more things you learn about Ted?

2

3 GRAMMAR FOCUS

Past tense

Where **were** you born?	I **was** born in South America.
Were you born in Brazil?	No, I **wasn't**. I **was** born in Argentina.
Where **did** you **grow** up?	I **grew** up in Buenos Aires.
When **did** you **move** here?	I **moved** here eight years ago, when I was in high school.
Did you **learn** Spanish in high school?	No, I **didn't**. I **studied** it in college.
Did you **go** to college in California?	Yes, I **did**. I **went** to college in Los Angeles.

A Complete these conversations. Then practice with a partner.

1. A: Could you tell me a little about yourself?
   Where .... you born?
   B: I .... born in South Korea.
   A: .... you grow up there?
   B: No, I .... I .... up in Canada.

2. A: Where .... you .... to high school?
   B: I .... to high school in Ecuador.

3. A: .... you study English when you ....
   a child?
   B: Yes, I ....
   A: How old .... you when you began to
   study English?
   B: I .... eleven years old.

B *Pair work* Take turns asking the questions in
part A. Give your own information when answering.

4 LISTENING

Listen to interviews with two immigrants to the
United States. Complete the chart.

	Yu Hong	Ajay
1. Where is he/she from?		
2. When did he/she move to the United States?	hace ~años	
3. What does he/she do now?		
4. What is difficult about being an immigrant?		
5. What does he/she miss the most?	Im make sup	

5 GETTING TO KNOW YOU

A *Pair work* Interview a classmate you don't know very well.
Ask questions like the ones below and take notes. Start like this:

A: Hi! My name's . . . .
B: Hello. I'm . . . . Nice to meet you.
A: Good to meet you, too. Could you tell me a little about yourself?
B: Sure. What do you want to know?
A: Well, where were you born?

Where were you born?	Did you study any foreign languages?
Did you grow up there?	When did you first study English?
Where did you go to elementary school?	When did you graduate?
Where did you go to high school?	How old were you when you moved to . . . ?

B *Class activity* Use your notes and introduce your partner
to the class. Start like this:

"I'd like to introduce Angela. She was born in Mexico, but she
grew up in a small town near Monterey, California."

---

6 WORD POWER *When I was a child . . . .*

A Complete the word map. Add one more
word to each category. Then compare with
a partner.

beach
bicycle
cat
collect comics
dog
paint
play chess
rabbit
scrapbook
soccer ball
summer camp
tree house

Pets
....
....
....
....

Hobbies
....
....
....
....

Childhood memories

Places
beach ....
....
....
....

Possessions
....
....
....
....

B *Pair work* Choose three words from
the word map and use them to describe
some of your childhood memories.

A: I played chess when I was in
   elementary school.
B: How well did you play?
A: I was pretty good.

4

7 CONVERSATION

A 📻 Listen and practice.

Jeff: Hey! Are these pictures of you when you were a kid?
Kim: Yeah. That's me in front of my uncle's beach house. When I was a kid, we used to spend two weeks there every summer.
Jeff: Wow, I bet that was fun!
Kim: Yeah. We always had a great time. Every day we used to get up early and walk along the beach. I had a great shell collection. In fact, I think it's still up in the attic!
Jeff: Hey, I used to collect shells, too, when I was a kid. But my parents threw them out!

B 📻 Listen to the rest of the conversation. What is Jeff's favorite childhood memory?

8 GRAMMAR FOCUS

Used to 📀

Used to *refers to something that you regularly did in the past but don't do anymore.*

When I was a kid, we **used to** stay at my uncle's beach house.

Did you **use to** have a hobby?
    Yes, I **used to** collect shells.

What games **did** you **use to** play?
    I **used to** play chess.

A Complete these sentences. Then compare with a partner.

1. In elementary school, I used to . . . .
2. I used to be . . . , but I'm not anymore.
3. When I was a kid, I used to play . . . .
4. After school, my best friend and I used to . . . .

B *Pair work* Write five more sentences about yourself using *used to.* Do you and your partner have anything in common?

9 PRONUNCIATION Used to

A  Listen and practice. Notice the pronunciation of **used to**.

When I was a child, I **used to** play the violin.
> I **used to** have a nickname.
> I **used to** have a pet.
> I **used to** play hide-and-seek.

B *Pair work* Practice the sentences you wrote in Exercise 8 again. Pay attention to the pronunciation of **used to**.

10 MEMORIES

A *Pair work* Add three questions to this list. Then take turns asking and answering the questions.

1. What's your favorite childhood memory?
2. What sports or games did you use to play when you were younger?
3. Did you use to have a nickname?
4. Where did you use to spend your vacations?
5. Did you ever have a part-time job?
6. ....
7. ....
8. ....

B *Class activity* Tell the class two interesting things about your partner.

11 WRITING

A Write about the things you used to do as a child. Use some of your ideas from Exercise 10.

> *When I was four years old, my family moved to Oregon.*
> *We had an old two-story house and a big yard to play in.*
> *My older brother and I used to play lots of games together.*
> *In the summer, my favorite outdoor game was hide-and-seek.*
> *It was both fun and scary because we . . . .*

interchange 1

Class profile
Find out about your classmates. Turn to page IC-2.

B *Group work* Take turns reading your compositions aloud. Answer any questions from the group.

12 *READING*

JoanChen

Do you know these film terms?
actor/actress   agent   director   film studio   producer   (leading) part

a scene from *The Last Emperor*

Joan Chen is famous both in China, where she grew up, and in the United States, where she now lives. How did Joan become a famous actress in two countries? It's an interesting story.

Joan Chen was born in Shanghai in 1961. When she was 14, some people from a film studio came to her school and chose her to study at the studio. She was happy about this chance, but mainly she liked the idea of getting out of school. Soon, however, she discovered that she really liked acting. At age 18, she won the Golden Rooster, China's top film award.

In the late 1970s, Joan's parents, who were doctors, moved to the United States. Joan joined them when she was 20 and went to college there. Her parents hoped she would study medicine. Instead, she majored in film and later looked for work as an actress. To work in the United States, Joan had to start all over again. She told Hollywood agents that she was an actress in China, but she only got some small parts in TV shows.

One day Joan went to speak to a director who was making a movie called *Tai-Pan*. The interview didn't go well. As she walked away, a man in a car noticed her. The man was Dino DeLaurentiis, the film's producer. He immediately offered her a leading part. A year later, she starred in Bernardo Bertolucci's *The Last Emperor* and was on her way to worldwide fame.

A Read the article. Then put the events in Joan Chen's life into the correct order (1–8).

.... won the Golden Rooster
.... appeared in *Tai-Pan*
.... left school and studied at a film studio
.... starred in *The Last Emperor*

.... studied film in college
.... moved to the United States
...1... was born in China in 1961
.... got her first part in a TV show

B *Group work* Talk about these questions.

1. Do parents and children often have different ideas about careers? How are their ideas different?
2. Why is it sometimes difficult for people who move to another country to keep doing the same work?

Caught in the rush

WORD POWER Compound nouns

A Match the nouns in columns A and B to make compound nouns. (More than one answer is possible.)

subway + entrance = subway entrance

A	B
subway	entrance
traffic	stop
bus	light
bicycle	station
stop	sign
parking	lane
street	stand
news	jam
taxi	space

a subway entrance

a traffic light

B *Pair work* How many compound nouns can you make beginning with these words?

police   telephone   fire   train

2 ## CONVERSATION

A 🔊 Listen and practice.

Lynn: Why is there never a bus when you want one?
Sam: Good question. There aren't enough buses on this route.
Lynn: Sometimes I feel like writing a letter to the paper.
Sam: Good idea. You should say that we need more subway lines, too.
Lynn: Yeah. There should be more public transportation in general.
Sam: And fewer cars! There's too much traffic.
Lynn: Say, is that our bus coming?
Sam: Yes, it is. But look. It's full!
Lynn: Oh, no! Let's go and get a cup of coffee. We can talk about this letter I'm going to write.

B 🔊 Listen to the rest of the conversation. What else is wrong with the transportation system in their city?

3 GRAMMAR FOCUS

> ### *Adverbs of quantity*
>
> | With countable nouns | With uncountable nouns |
> |---|---|
> | There are **too many** cars. | There is **too much** traffic. |
> | There are**n't enough** buses. | There is**n't enough** parking. |
> | We need **more** subway lines. | We need **more** public transportation. |
> | There should be **fewer** cars. | There should be **less** pollution. |

A Complete these statements about transportation problems. Then compare with a partner. (More than one answer may be possible.)

1. There are .... police officers.
2. There should be .... cars in the city.
3. There is .... public transportation.
4. The government needs to build .... highways.
5. There should be .... noise.
6. We should have .... public parking garages.
7. There is .... air pollution in the city.
8. There are .... cars parked on the streets.

B *Group work* Complete these statements about the city you are living in. Then compare with others.

1. The city needs to provide more . . . .
2. We have too many . . . .
3. There's too much . . . .
4. There should be fewer . . . .
5. We don't have enough . . . .
6. There should be less . . . .

4 LISTENING

A 💿 Listen to someone talk about how Singapore has tried to solve its traffic problems. Check (✓) True or False for each statement.

	True	False
1. Motorists are never allowed to drive into the business district.	☐	☐
2. People need a special certificate to be able to buy a car.	☐	☐
3. Cars cost much more than they do in the United States and Canada.	☐	☐
4. Public transportation still needs to be improved.	☐	☐

B 💿 Listen again. For the statements that you marked false, write the correct information.

C *Class activity* Could the solutions adopted in Singapore work in your city? Why or why not?

5 YOU BE THE JUDGE!

A *Group work* How would you rate the transportation services in your city? Complete the chart. Give each item a rating from 1 to 5.

1 = terrific   2 = good   3 = average (OK)   4 = needs improvement   5 = terrible

.... the train system	.... taxi service	.... the bus system
.... facilities for pedestrians	.... the subway system	.... parking

B *Class activity* Explain your ratings to the class.

"We gave taxi service a rating of 4. We think the city needs more taxis and cheaper fares. Also, taxi drivers should be more polite."

interchange 2

Making the city better

Suggest ways to improve a city. Turn to page IC-3.

6 WRITING

Write a paragraph about transportation in your city.

> *Public transportation is good in my city. We have an excellent bus system. The traffic moves quickly, except at rush hour. However, we need more public parking. There aren't enough parking spaces downtown, so it always takes too much time to find a space.*

7 SNAPSHOT

Special modes of **transportation**

ferry	magnetic levitation (maglev) train	gondola	tuk-tuk	cable car
Hong Kong, China	Berlin, Germany	Venice, Italy	Bangkok, Thailand	San Francisco, California, USA

Source: *World Book Encyclopedia*

Talk about these questions.

Have you used any of these kinds of transportation?
Are there any unusual forms of transportation in your city or country?
What kinds of transportation do you usually use?

8 CONVERSATION

A 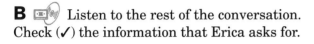 Listen and practice.

Erica: Excuse me. Could you tell me where the bank is?
Man: There's one upstairs, across from the duty-free shop.
Erica: Oh, thanks. Do you know what time it opens?
Man: It should be open now. It opens at 8:00 A.M.
Erica: Good. And can you tell me how often the buses leave for the city?
Man: You need to check at the transportation counter. It's right down the hall.
Erica: OK. And just one more thing. Do you know where the nearest restroom is?
Man: Right behind you, ma'am. See that sign?
Erica: Oh. Thanks a lot.

B 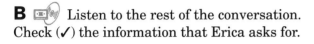 Listen to the rest of the conversation.
Check (✓) the information that Erica asks for.

☒ the cost of a taxi to the city   ☐ the location of a cash machine
☐ the location of the taxi stand   ☐ the location of a restaurant

9 GRAMMAR FOCUS

Indirect questions from Wh-questions

Wh-questions with be	*Indirect questions*
Where is the bank?	Could you tell me **where the bank is?**
Where is the taxi stand?	Do you know **where the taxi stand is?**
Wh-questions with do *or* did	*Indirect questions*
How often do the buses leave for the city?	Can you tell me **how often the buses leave for the city?**
When did Flight 566 arrive?	Do you know **when Flight 566 arrived?**
What time does the duty-free shop open?	Do you know **what time the duty-free shop opens?**

A Write indirect questions using these Wh-questions.
Then compare with a partner.

1. How much does a newspaper cost?
2. Where is the nearest cash machine?
3. What time do the banks open?
4. How often do the buses come?
5. Where can you get a good hamburger?
6. How late do the nightclubs stay open?

B *Pair work* Take turns asking the questions you wrote in part A.
Give your own information when answering.

A: Do you know how often the buses come?
B: Every half hour.

10 PRONUNCIATION Question intonation

A 🔊 Listen and practice. Wh-questions usually have falling intonation. Indirect questions usually have rising intonation.

What time does the duty-free shop open?

Can you tell me what time the duty-free shop opens?

Where is the taxi stand?

Do you know where the taxi stand is?

B Practice these questions. Pay attention to question intonation.

Where is Adam Street?
Could you tell me where Adam Street is?
What time does the department store open?
Do you know what time the department store opens?

11 TOURISTS

A *Pair work* What would a tourist visiting your city ask about? Think of six questions about transportation, accommodations, sightseeing, and other services in your city.

B *Group work* Take turns asking and answering your questions.

A: Can you tell me where the Golden Pavilion is?
B: Let me think. Oh, yes, it's . . . .

useful expressions

Let me think. Oh, yes, ...
I'm not really sure,
    but I think . . . .
Sorry, I don't know.
It's close to/near . . . .
It's on the corner of . . . .
It's next to . . . .

Golden Pavilion, Kyoto, Japan

12 READING

Stuck in an Airport?
What to do . . .

What do people usually do while they're waiting in an airport?

Many people are upset when their flight is delayed. Not only do they have to change their schedule but, even worse, they have to wait in an airport! There's no need to be upset, though. Airports are much better places these days than most people realize.

Honolulu Airport, Hawaii

- **Belief:** Airport food is bad – as bad as airplane food.

- **Reality:** Airports have fine international cuisine – from fresh seafood in London to Korean barbecue in Honolulu. And you can stock up on something to have for later – for example, cheese and caviar in Paris.

Schiphol Airport, Amsterdam

Heathrow Airport, London

- **Belief:** Shopping in airports is great, that is, if you need a T-shirt.

- **Reality:** In Amsterdam, you can buy anything from perfume to diamonds. In El Paso, Texas, you can buy antique knives or regional art. The art is so interesting that some people fly to El Paso just to visit the airport gallery. And Singapore's airport is known for some of the best shopping in the world!

- **Belief:** Airports make people uncomfortable and tense.

- **Reality:** The airport at Honolulu has peaceful gardens. Pittsburgh has a meditation room: When you walk in, relaxing music comes on and pictures of clouds are projected on the walls. If you prefer exercise, hotels at the airports in Los Angeles, Dallas, and many other cities have fitness centers that anyone can use.

So, the next time you're stuck in an airport, have some fun!

A Read the article. In which airport can you do the following? Write the letter of the correct place.

1. meditate surrounded by music and clouds ....
2. eat Korean barbecue ....
3. buy an interesting painting ....
4. exercise in a fitness center ....
5. buy a diamond ....
6. visit one of the world's best shopping places ....

a. Amsterdam
b. Dallas
c. Singapore
d. Honolulu
e. Pittsburgh
f. El Paso

B *Group work* Talk about these questions.

1. Which airport mentioned in the article would you prefer to wait in? Why?
2. Imagine your flight is delayed. What would you prefer to do: eat, shop, or relax? Anything else?

3 Time for a change!

1 WORD POWER Houses and apartments

A These adjectives are used to describe houses and apartments. Which words are positive? Which are negative? Write **P** or **N** next to each word.

cramped

comfortable

bright	..P..	dingy	....	private	....
comfortable	....	expensive	....	quiet	....
convenient	....	huge	....	safe	....
cramped	....	inconvenient	....	shabby	....
dangerous	....	modern	....	small	....
dark	....	noisy	....	spacious	....

B *Pair work* Tell your partner two positive and two negative features about your house or apartment.

"My apartment is very dark and a little cramped. However, it's in a safe neighborhood and it's very private."

2 CONVERSATION Apartment hunting

A 🔲📻 Listen and practice.

Mr. Dean: What do you think?

Mrs. Dean: Well, it has just as many bedrooms as the last apartment. And the living room is huge.

Jenny: But the bedrooms are too small. And there isn't enough closet space for my clothes.

Mr. Dean: And it's not as cheap as the last apartment we saw.

Mrs. Dean: But that apartment was dark and dingy. And it was in a dangerous neighborhood.

Mr. Dean: Let's see if the real estate agent has something else to show us.

B 🔲📻 Listen to the Deans talk about another apartment. What does Jenny like about it? What doesn't she like?

14

3 GRAMMAR FOCUS

Evaluations and comparisons

Evaluations with adjectives
The kitchen is**n't** big **enough**.
The living room is **too** small.

Evaluations with nouns
There are**n't enough** bedrooms.
There is**n't enough** closet space.

Comparisons with adjectives
It's **not as** cheap **as** the last apartment.
It's **almost as** cheap (**as** the last apartment).

Comparisons with nouns
It doesn't have **as many** bedrooms **as** the last apartment.
It has **just as many** bedrooms (**as** the last apartment).

A Read the opinions about these apartments. Then rephrase the opinions using the words in parentheses.

Spacious, modern apartment
2 bedrooms, 1 bathroom; very private;
located outside the city; 2-car garage;
$800 per month.

Older, small apartment
2 bedrooms, 2 bathrooms; located
downtown, by the commuter train;
1 parking space; $800 per month.

Apartment 1

1. There are only a few windows. (not enough)
2. It's not bright enough. (too)
3. It has only one bathroom. (not enough)
4. It's not convenient enough. (too)

Apartment 2

5. It's not spacious enough. (too)
6. It's too old. (not enough)
7. It isn't quiet enough. (too)
8. There's only one parking space. (not enough)

"There aren't enough windows."

B Write comparisons of the apartments using the words below and *as . . . as.*
Then compare with a partner.

Apartment 1	*Apartment 2*
bright	big
bedrooms	expensive
bathrooms	modern

Apartment 1 isn't as bright as Apartment 2.

C *Pair work* Compare living in an apartment to living in a house.
Which would you prefer to live in?

A: A house is not as expensive as an apartment.
B: Yes, but an apartment is too small for a large family.

4 PRONUNCIATION *Sentence stress*

A 🎧 Listen and practice. Stress the words in a sentence that carry the most important information.

The apártment isn't **bíg** enough.   There **áre**n't enough **cló**sets.
The **kít**chen is **tóo** cramped.   There **ís**n't enough **líght.**

B *Pair work* Practice the sentences you wrote in part A of Exercise 3.
Pay attention to sentence stress.

5 LISTENING

A 🎧 Listen to three people call about apartment advertisements.
Check (✓) the words that best describe each apartment.

1.		2.		3.	
☐ quiet	☑ noisy	☐ spacious	☑ small	☐ expensive	☑ reasonable
☑ spacious	☐ cramped	☑ convenient	☐ inconvenient	☑ safe	☐ dangerous
☐ modern	☑ old	☑ quiet	☐ noisy	☑ dark	☑ light

B 🎧 Listen again. Do you think each caller is going to rent
the apartment? Why or why not?

6 SNAPSHOT

Based on interviews with adults between 18 and 50

Talk about these questions.

Which of these things would you like to do? Give some examples.
What other things would you like to change about your life? Why?

7 CONVERSATION *Making wishes*

A Listen and practice.

Brian: So where are you working now, Terry?
Terry: Oh, I'm still at the bank. I don't like it, though.
Brian: That's too bad. Why not?
Terry: Well, it's boring, and it doesn't pay very well.
Brian: I know what you mean. I don't like my job either. I wish I could find a better job.
Terry: Actually, I don't want to work at all anymore. I wish I had a lot of money so I could retire now.
Brian: Hmm, how old are you, Terry?
Terry: Uh, twenty-six.

B Listen to the rest of the conversation. What other changes would Brian and Terry like to make?

8 GRAMMAR FOCUS

Wish

Wish *is followed by past tense forms but refers to the present.*

Fact	Wish
I don't like my job.	I **wish** (that) I **could find** a better job. I **wish** I **worked** somewhere else.
I live with my parents.	I **wish** I **lived** in my own apartment. I **wish** I **didn't live** with my parents.
Life is difficult.	I **wish** it **were** * easier. I **wish** it **weren't** so difficult.

*After wish, were *is used with* I, he, she, *and* it.

Write a response using *wish* for each statement. Then compare with a partner. (More than one answer is possible.)

1. My class is boring.
2. I have to take the bus to work every day.
3. Our apartment is too small.
4. I have too much homework.
5. I'm not in good shape.
6. I'm single.
7. I don't have enough money.
8. I don't have any free time.

> *I wish my class were more interesting.*
> *I wish that I could take another class.*

9 LISTENING

A 📼 Listen to four people talk about things they wish they could change. Check (✓) the topic each person is talking about.

Topic			
1. ☐ apartment	**2.** ☐ leisure	**3.** ☐ skills	**4.** ☐ interests
☐ job	☐ school	☐ hobbies	☐ appearance

B 📼 Listen again. What change would each person like to make? Why?

interchange 3

Wishful thinking
Find out about your classmates' wishes. Turn to page IC-4.

10 TIME FOR A CHANGE

A What do you wish were different about these situations? Write down your wishes. Then compare with a partner.

your appearance   your school or job   your skills
your family   your home   your free time

B *Group work* Choose two of your wishes from part A. Take turns talking about your wishes and how you would make the necessary changes.

A: I wish I could change my job.
B: Really?
A: Yes. I'd like to be a musician.
C: A musician? Wow!
A: I'd like to play the guitar in a rock band. I could take guitar lessons. And then . . . .

11 WRITING

A Write about one of your wishes from Exercise 10.

> *I wish I had more free time. I take classes all day, and I have a part-time job in the evening. At home, I spend my time studying or doing chores around the house. I'd like to have more time to read and go out with my friends.*

B *Pair work* Take turns reading your compositions with a partner. Give your partner suggestions for making the change.

12 *READING*

Dreams Can Come True

Do you know anyone who made a big change in his or her lifestyle?

At the age of 40, Tom Bloch was the head of H&R Block, a huge company that helps people prepare their tax forms. He was very successful. Although Bloch earned a lot of money, he wasn't very happy: He spent too much time at work and didn't have enough time to spend with his family. Suddenly, he left H&R Block and became a teacher in a poor neighborhood. "I wanted to . . . help people who didn't have the opportunities I had," Bloch explained.

Learning to control the students was hard at first. But the rewards – helping children and hearing students say he's their favorite teacher – are great. And Bloch is able to spend more time with his family.

the Neale family

Tom Bloch with his students

For eleven years, Tom Neale worked as a lawyer, and his wife, Mel, worked as a teacher; they saved every penny they could. Finally, they had enough money to buy a boat. That was seventeen years ago, and, except for occasional stops, they have been at sea ever since.

For the Neales and their two daughters, the difficulties of their lifestyle are very real: There's not much money, so meals are often rice and beans (and fish!). Storms are dangerous, especially when the boat is far from land. But Tom Neale says overcoming dangers together as a family is one of the rewards of their way of life. Another, he says, is "seeing the starfish on the bottom of the sea in the moonlight."

A Read the article. What do these people do now? What is one difficulty with their new lifestyles? What is one reward? Complete the chart.

	What they do now	Difficulty	Reward
1. Tom Bloch	....	....	....
2. the Neales	....	....	....

B *Group work* Talk about these questions.

1. Who do you think made the more difficult change in lifestyle, Tom Bloch or the Neales? Explain your answer.
2. Would you like to be one of the Neales' children? Why or why not?
3. What are some reasons people – those in the article and others – change their lifestyles?
4. Would you like to change your lifestyle? If so, how?

1 SNAPSHOT

Favorite Ethnic Dishes

Brazil
Feijoada
A traditional dish made of black beans, garlic, spices, and pork.

Thailand
Mee Krob
Crispy fried noodles with shrimp and chicken.

China
Won Ton Soup
Chicken soup with pork-filled dumplings.

Latin America
Ceviche
Raw seafood marinated in lime juice and chili peppers.

Sources: *Fodor's South America, Fodor's Southeast Asia, World Book Encyclopedia*

Talk about these questions.

Have you ever tried any of these dishes? Which ones would you like to try?
What other ethnic food can you try in your city?
What are three popular dishes in your country?

2 CONVERSATION

A 🔊 Listen and practice.

Kathy: Hey, this sounds good – snails with garlic! Have you ever eaten snails?
John: No, I haven't.
Kathy: Oh, they're delicious! I had them last time. Like to try some?
John: No, thanks. They sound strange.
Waitress: Have you decided on an appetizer yet?
Kathy: Yes. I'll have the snails, please.
Waitress: And you, sir?
John: I think I'll have the fried brains.
Kathy: Fried brains? Now that really sounds strange!

B 🔊 Listen to the rest of the conversation. How did John like the fried brains? What else did he order?

3 PRONUNCIATION Reduced forms

 Listen and practice. Notice how **did you** and **have you** are pronounced in these questions.

Did you skip breakfast this morning?
Did you cook your own dinner last night?

Have you ever tried Indian food?
Have you ever eaten snails?

4 GRAMMAR FOCUS

Simple past vs. present perfect

Simple past: completed events at a definite time in the past	Present perfect: events within a time period up to the present

Did you **eat** snails at the restaurant last night?
    No, I **didn't**.
Did you **go** out for dinner on Saturday?
    Yes, I **did**.
	Have you ever **eaten** snails?
	    No, I **haven't**.
	Have you **been** to a French restaurant?
	    Yes, I **have**.

I **went** to a Korean restaurant last week.	I've **never been** to a Greek restaurant.

A Complete these conversations. Then practice with a partner. (See the appendix for help with verb forms.)

1. A: Have you ever .... (be) to a picnic at the beach?
   B: Yes, I .... It was fun!

2. A: Did you .... (have) dinner at home last night?
   B: No, I .... I .... (go) out for dinner.

3. A: Have you .... (try) sushi?
   B: No, I .... , but I'd like to.

4. A: Did you .... (have) breakfast this morning?
   B: Yes, I .... I .... (eat) a huge breakfast.

5. A: Have you ever .... (eat) at a Mexican restaurant?
   B: Yes, I .... The food was delicious!

B *Pair work* Take turns asking and answering the questions in part A. Give your own information. Pay attention to the pronunciation of **did you** and **have you**.

5 LISTENING

Listen to six people ask questions about food and drink in a restaurant. Check (✓) the item that each person is talking about.

1. ☐ water   2. ☐ coffee   3. ☐ soup   4. ☐ coffee   5. ☐ cake   6. ☐ the check
   ☐ bread   ☐ the meal   ☐ pasta   ☐ the meat   ☐ coffee   ☐ the menu

6 BUSYBODIES

Pair work Ask your partner these questions and four more
of your own. Then ask follow-up questions.

Did you . . . ?

make your own breakfast this morning
go out for dinner last week
eat a big lunch yesterday

Have you ever . . . ?

tried frog's legs
been on a diet
cooked a large dinner for some friends

A: Did you make your own breakfast this morning?
B: Yes, I did.
A: What did you make?
B: I made scrambled eggs.

interchange 4

Risky business
Find out some interesting
facts about your
classmates.
Turn to page
IC-5.

7 WORD POWER Cooking methods

A How do you cook these foods? Check (✓) the methods that
are most common in your country. Then compare with a partner.

bake   fry   roast   boil   barbecue   steam

Methods	Foods								
	fish	shrimp	eggs	chicken	beef	potatoes	onions	eggplant	bananas
bake	☐	☐	☐	☐	☐	☐	☐	☐	☐
fry	☐	☐	☐	☐	☐	☐	☐	☐	☐
roast	☐	☐	☐	☐	☐	☐	☐	☐	☐
boil	☐	☐	☐	☐	☐	☐	☐	☐	☐
barbecue	☐	☐	☐	☐	☐	☐	☐	☐	☐
steam	☐	☐	☐	☐	☐	☐	☐	☐	☐

B What's your favorite way to cook the foods in part A?

A: I usually like to steam fish.
B: I prefer to bake it.

8 CONVERSATION

A 🔊 Listen and practice.

Kate: What's your favorite snack?

Jim: Oh, it's a sandwich with peanut butter, honey, and a banana. It's really delicious!

Kate: Ugh! I've never heard of that! How do you make it?

Jim: Well, first, you take two slices of bread and spread peanut butter on them. Then cut a banana into small pieces and put them on one of the slices of bread. Finally, pour some honey over the bananas and put the other slice of bread on top. Yum!

Kate: Yuck! It sounds awful!

B 🔊 Listen to the rest of the conversation. What is Kate's favorite snack? Would you like to try it? Why or why not?

9 GRAMMAR FOCUS

> **Sequence adverbs** 🔊
>
> **First,** spread peanut butter on two slices of bread.
> **Then** cut a banana into small pieces.
> **Next,** put the pieces of banana on one slice of bread.
> **After that,** pour honey over the bananas.
> **Finally,** put the other slice of bread on top.

A Here's a recipe for barbecued kebobs. Look at the pictures and number the sentences from 1 to 5. Then add a sequence adverb to each step.

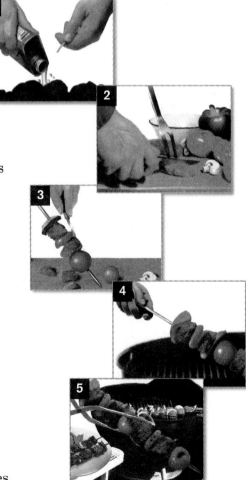

[3] .... put the meat and vegetables on the skewers.

[1] .... put charcoal in the barbecue and light it with lighter fluid.

[5] .... take the kebobs off the barbecue and enjoy!

[4] .... put the kebobs on the barbecue and cook for 10 to 15 minutes, turning them over from time to time.

[2] .... cut up some meat and vegetables and put them in a bowl with your favorite barbecue marinade. Marinate for 20 minutes.

B *Pair work* Cover the recipe and look only at the pictures. Explain each step of the recipe to your partner.

10 TEMPTING SNACKS

A 🔊 Listen to people explain how to make these snacks.
Which snack are they talking about? Number the photos (1–4).

guacamole dip

toasted bagel

pizza

popcorn

B *Pair work* Choose one of the recipes you heard about in part A.
Can you remember how to make it? Compare with your partner.

C *Group work* Take turns describing how to make your favorite
snack. Then tell the class about the most interesting one.

A: What's your favorite snack?
B: It's . . . .
C: What ingredients do you need to make it?
B: You need . . . .
A: How do you make it?
B: Well, first, you . . . . After that, ... Next, ... Then . . . .

11 WRITING Recipes

A Write a recipe for an interesting dish. First, list the
ingredients you need. Then describe how to make the dish.

> *This recipe is for chicken curry. For this dish, you need chicken, coconut milk, ...*
> *First, cut up the chicken. Then fry the chicken pieces in oil . . . .*

B *Group work* Exchange recipes and read them. Is there a recipe you would like to try? Why?

12 READING

Eating for Energy

Do you know anything about this food pyramid? What does it show?

Many professional sports teams have recently added a new member to their organization – a nutritionist. That's because athletes have become aware that food affects performance. You don't have to be an athlete to notice this effect. If you've ever skipped breakfast and then tried to clean the house, you know that you need food for energy. Here are some tips about eating to increase your physical performance:

▲ **Eat enough food.** Your body needs a certain number of calories each day. If you're too thin, you'll often feel tired and you'll be more likely to get sick.

▲ **Read the labels on food products.** This information will tell you how nutritious the foods are.

▲ **Avoid eating foods that are high in simple carbohydrates, that is, sugars.** A chocolate bar will first give you energy, but then it will leave you feeling even more tired.

▲ **Eat a balanced diet, one that includes complex carbohydrates, protein, and fat.** Use the food pyramid to help you decide how much to eat of each type of food. Complex carbohydrates provide the body with "fuel." They are found in fruits and vegetables, and in bread, rice, pasta, and other foods made from grains. The body uses protein to build muscles, and it uses fat to absorb the vitamins in food. Protein and fat are found in foods like milk, cheese, meat, fish, and eggs. Too much fat, however, can be harmful.

A Read the article and look at the food pyramid. Then check (✓) True or False. For the statements that you marked false, write the correct information.

	True	False
1. You shouldn't eat foods that are high in complex carbohydrates.	☐	☐
2. Fruits and vegetables are a good source of protein.	☐	☐
3. A person should eat more carbohydrates than fat or protein.	☐	☐
4. If you're too thin, you might get sick easily.	☐	☐

B *Group work* Talk about these questions.

1. Which of the tips in the article do you already follow?
2. What do you eat in a typical day? Is your diet balanced? What do you need to eat more of? less of?
3. Can you think of a time when eating (or not eating) affected your performance? What happened?

Review of Units 1-4

1 HOW TIMES HAVE CHANGED!

A *Group work* Talk about how family life has changed in the last fifty years in your country. Ask and answer questions like these:

How big were families fifty years ago?
What kinds of homes did people live in then?
What kinds of jobs did men use to have?
  And what about women?
How were schools different?
How much did people use to earn?
What kinds of machines and appliances did people use?

B *Class activity* Compare answers. Do you think life was better in the old days? Why or why not?

2 CITY PLANNERS

A *Pair work* How would you make your city or town a better place for young people? Make suggestions.

A: How would you make the city better for young people?
B: Well, there should be more free concerts in the summer.
A: You're right. And there aren't enough parks.

B *Group work* Compare your ideas. Which suggestions do you think are best?

3 LISTENING

Listen to people ask for information. Check (✓) the correct response.

1. ☐ It's just around the corner.
   ☐ Yes, it closes at three.

2. ☐ Yes, it does.
   ☐ The next one is in ten minutes.

3. ☐ On the corner of Main and 15th.
   ☐ At nine o'clock in the morning.

4. ☐ It's in the shopping center on King Street.
   ☐ Not until two o'clock.

5. ☐ Yes, in the Fairmont Hotel on Main Street.
   ☐ Yes, I do.

6. ☐ By bus.
   ☐ On the corner of Orange and Dewey.

4 COMPUTER SHOPPING

Pair work Look at these ads for computers. Make comparisons using *as . . . as*. Which computer would you buy?

"Computer 2 isn't as old as computer 1."

For sale: Used IBM computer (4 yrs old). 8 MB of memory. 13 inch screen. $2000. Price includes three software programs. **Call 638-2825.**

FOR SALE:
Used IBM computer (2 yrs old). 16 MB of memory. 20 inch screen. $2000. Price includes two software programs. **Call 638-7693.**

5 HOME IMPROVEMENTS

A Make a list of five things you wish you could change about your house or apartment.

B *Pair work* Compare your lists. Give at least one reason for each wish.

A: I wish I had a bigger bedroom. It's too small for all my things.
B: I know what you mean. I wish . . . .

6 TALKING ABOUT FOOD

A Complete the sentences with information about food.

1. I have never tried .... food.
2. I have tried .... food, but I don't really like it.
3. The most unusual thing I have ever eaten is ....
4. The worst food I have ever tried is ....
5. A dish I have never tried but would like to try is ....
6. I have often cooked ....

B *Pair work* Compare sentences with a partner. Ask and answer follow-up questions.

A: I've never tried Russian food.
B: Oh, I have. It's delicious.
A: What is a common Russian dish?

C *Pair work* Describe how to make a food that you like to cook.

"I like to cook . . . . To make it, first you . . . . Then . . . . Next, ..."

Going places

1 SNAPSHOT

what people like to do on vacation

Discover something new
- [ ] take language, cooking, or sailing lessons
- [ ] join an archaeological dig

Take an exciting trip
- [ ] visit a foreign country
- [ ] travel through their own country by car or train

Enjoy nature
- [ ] go camping, hiking, or fishing
- [ ] relax at the beach

Stay home
- [ ] catch up on reading
- [ ] fix up or redecorate the house

Based on information from *U.S. News and World Report* and *American Demographics*

Complete these tasks.

Which of the activities above do you like to do on vacation? Check (✓) the activities.
Make a list of other activities you like to do on vacation. Then compare with a partner.

2 CONVERSATION

A Listen and practice

Julia: I'm so excited! We have two weeks off! What are you going to do?
Nancy: I'm not sure. I guess I'll just stay home. Maybe I'll catch up on my reading. What about you? Any plans?
Julia: Well, my parents have rented a condominium in Florida. I'm going to take long walks along the beach every day and do lots of swimming.
Nancy: Sounds great!
Julia: Say, why don't you come with us? We have plenty of room.
Nancy: Do you mean it? I'd love to!

B *Class activity* Have you ever taken a vacation at the beach? What kinds of things can you do there?

3 GRAMMAR FOCUS

Future with be going to and will

Use be going to + verb to talk about plans you've decided on. Use will + verb with maybe, probably, I guess, or I think to talk about possible plans before you've made a decision.

Where **are** you **going to go**?	I**'m going to go** to the beach.	I'm not sure. **Maybe I'll catch up** on my reading.
	I**'m** not **going to take** a vacation.	**I probably won't take** a vacation this year.
What **are** you **going to do**?	I**'m going to do** lots of swimming.	**I guess** I'**ll** just **stay** home.
		I don't know. **I think** I'**ll go** camping.

A Complete the conversation with appropriate forms of *be going to* or *will*. Then compare with a partner.

A: Have you made any vacation plans?
B: Well, I've decided on one thing –
 I .... go camping.
A: That's great! For how long?
B: I .... be away for a week.
 I only have five days of vacation.
A: So, when are you leaving?
B: I'm not sure. I .... probably leave
 around the end of May.
A: And where .... you .... go?
B: I haven't thought about that yet. I guess
 I .... go to one of the national parks.
A: That sounds like fun.
B: Yeah. Maybe I .... go
 hiking and do some fishing.
A: .... you .... rent a camper?
B: I'm not sure. Actually, I probably ....
 rent a camper – it's too expensive.
A: .... you .... go with anyone?
B: No. I need some time alone.
 I .... travel by myself.

B Have you thought about your next vacation? Write answers
to these questions. (If you already have plans, use *be going to*.
If you don't have fixed plans, use *will*.)

1. How are you going to spend your next vacation?
 Are you going to go anywhere?
2. When are you going to take your vacation?
3. How long are you going to be on vacation?
4. What are you going to do?
5. Is anyone going to travel with you?

I'm going to take my next vacation . . . .
OR
I'm not sure. Maybe I'll . . . .

C *Group work* Take turns telling the group about your vacation plans.
Use the information you wrote in part B.

4 *WRITING* Itineraries

Write about the trip you planned in Exercise 3
or another trip you are going to take.

Borobodur in Central Java

> *Next summer, I'm going to travel to Indonesia with*
> *my family. We're going to visit Borobodur in Central*
> *Java. It's one of the biggest temples in the world.*
> *And we'll probably visit several other temples nearby. . . .*

5 *LISTENING*

A Listen to Judy, Paul, and Brenda describe their summer plans.
Check (✓) the correct piece of information about each person's plans.

Who . . . ?	1. Judy	2. Paul	3. Brenda
is going to learn about a different culture	☐	☐	☐
will probably visit several different countries	☐	☐	☐
probably won't take a vacation	☐	☑	☐
is going to lie on the beach	☐	☑	☐
is going to do something exciting and a little dangerous	☑	☐	☐

B Listen again. What is the main reason for each person's choice?

6 *WORD POWER* Travel

A Complete the chart. Then add one more word to each category.

backpack   first-aid kit   overnight bag   shorts   vaccination
cash   hiking boots   passport   suitcase   visa
credit card   medication   plane ticket   traveler's checks windbreaker

Clothing	Money	Health	Travel documents	Luggage
....	....	....	....	....
....	....	....	....	....
....	....	....	....	....

B *Pair work* What are the five most important items you need for these vacations:
a trip to a foreign country? a rafting trip? a mountain-climbing expedition?

7 CONVERSATION

A  Listen and practice.

Lucy: Hey, Mom. I want to backpack around Europe this summer. What do you think?

Mom: Backpack around Europe? That sounds dangerous! You shouldn't go by yourself. You ought to go with someone.

Lucy: Yes, I've thought of that.

Mom: And you'd better talk to your father first.

Lucy: I already did. He thinks it's a great idea. He wants to come with me!

B *Class activity* Would you like to backpack around Europe? Which countries would you like to visit? Why?

8 GRAMMAR FOCUS

Modals for necessity and suggestion

Describing necessity	Giving suggestions
You **have to** get a passport.	You**'d better** talk to your father.
You **must** get a visa for some countries.	You **ought to** go with someone.
You **need to** take money.	You **should** take warm clothes.
For some countries, you **don't have to** get any vaccinations.	You **shouldn't** go by yourself.

A Give advice to someone who is thinking of taking a vacation abroad. Then compare with a partner.

"You must get a passport."
"You shouldn't pack too many clothes."

1. . . . get a passport.
2. . . . pack too many clothes.
3. . . . buy a round-trip plane ticket.
4. . . . make hotel reservations.
5. . . . get a vaccination.
6. . . . check the weather.
7. . . . carry lots of cash.
8. . . . get traveler's checks.
9. . . . take a lot of luggage.
10. . . . check on visas.
11. . . . carry your wallet in your back pocket.
12. . . . take identification with you.

B *Group work* Give four more pieces of advice.

9 PRONUNCIATION Ought to *and* have to

A Listen and practice. Notice the pronunciation of **ought to** and **have to** in these sentences.

You **ought to** take a credit card.
You **ought to** go in June.

You **have to** get a passport.
You **have to** get a visa.

B *Pair work* Write two sentences using *ought to* and two sentences using *have to*. Then practice them with a partner. Pay attention to pronunciation.

10 DREAM VACATION

A *Pair work* You won some money in a lottery. Plan an interesting trip around the world. Discuss these questions and others of your own. Make notes.

Where are we going to start from?
What time of the year should we travel?
How are we going to travel?
What countries and cities should we visit?
How long should we spend in each place?
Where are we going to stay?
What are we planning to do and see there?
How much money do we have to take?
What do we need to take with us?

B *Group work* Compare your plans. Which trip sounds the most exciting?

11 LISTENING Tourist tips

A spokesperson from the New York City Visitors and Convention Bureau is giving advice to visitors. What are four things people should do to make their visit to New York City safe and pleasant?

Advice
1. ....
2. ....
3. ....
4. ....

interchange 5

Fun vacations
Decide between two vacations. Student A turns to page IC-6. Student B turns to page IC-8.

12 *READING*

Getting more for less when you travel

Do you know how to get inexpensive airline and train tickets? hotel accommodations?

On a recent flight, Laura was chatting happily with the woman in the next seat – until the conversation turned to fares. The woman, who bought her ticket two months in advance, paid $109. Laura paid the full fare of $457. She decided that next time she would find out how to travel for less.

Here are some ways to travel for less:

traveling by train in Europe

Cheap airplane tickets. To fly for less money, you can buy non-refundable plane tickets two or three months before your trip. The cheapest way to fly is as a courier. In return for delivering a package for a courier company, you get a plane ticket that costs as little as one-quarter of the regular fare – or even less if the company needs someone at the last minute. Recently, a courier flew round trip from Los Angeles to Tokyo for $100; a regular ticket cost around $1,800.

Train passes. If you're going to do a lot of traveling by train, a train pass will save you money. Buying a single pass gives you unlimited travel for a period of time. Train passes can be especially useful in India, which has the world's largest rail system; in Japan, where trains are fast and convenient; and in Europe, where trains go to over 30,000 cities.

a hostel in Germany

Hostels. Hostels used to provide cheap accommodations – in dormitories – for people under the age of 25. Nowadays, hostels don't have any age requirements. They're not only cheap ($8–$17 a night) but a great way to meet people. Hostels are often in interesting places – a castle in Germany, a lighthouse in California, a one-room schoolhouse in the wilderness of Australia. And sometimes hostels have luxuries like swimming pools.

A In your own words, restate some of the information from the article using the phrases below.

1. 25% of the normal fare
2. $100 instead of $1,800
3. more than 30,000 cities
4. younger than 25
5. $17 or less

"Fly as a courier. You can buy your plane ticket for one-quarter of the normal fare."

B *Pair work* Talk about these questions. Give reasons for your answers.

1. Would you want to travel as an air courier? take a long train trip? stay in a hostel?
2. What advice would you give someone who wants to travel for less in your country? Which hotels, restaurants, means of transportation, and stores would you recommend?

6 Sure. No problem!

1 SNAPSHOT

Common complaints of families with teenagers

Parents about teens:

My kids . . .

☞ don't help around the house.
☞ don't listen to my advice.
☞ have strange friends.
☞ dress badly and have ugly hairstyles.
☞ watch too much TV.
☞ don't study enough.

Teens about parents:

My parents . . .

☞ nag about chores and homework.
☞ don't like my friends.
☞ criticize my appearance.
☞ don't respect my privacy.
☞ always tell me what to do.
☞ don't listen to my opinions.

Based on information from America Online's Parent Resource Site

Talk about these questions.

Have you ever heard parents or children make these complaints? Which ones?
Have you ever had any complaints like these about family members?

2 CONVERSATION *Making requests*

A 📼 Listen and practice.

Mr. Field: Jason . . . Jason! Turn down the TV a little, please.
Jason: Oh, but this is my favorite program!
Mr. Field: I know. But it's very loud.
Jason: OK. I'll turn it down.
Mr. Field: That's better. Thanks.
Mrs. Field: Lisa, please pick up your things. They're all over the living room floor.
Lisa: In a minute, Mom. I'm on the phone.
Mrs. Field: OK. But do it as soon as you hang up.
Lisa: Sure. No problem!
Mrs. Field: Goodness! Were we like this when we were kids?
Mr. Field: Definitely!

B 📼 Listen to the rest of the conversation. What complaints do Jason and Lisa have about their parents?

3 GRAMMAR FOCUS

Two-part verbs; will *for responding to requests* 🔊

With nouns	With pronouns	Requests and responses
Turn down the TV. **Turn** the TV **down**.	**Turn** it **down**.	Please turn down the music. OK. I'**ll** turn it down.
Pick up your things. **Pick** your things **up**.	**Pick** them **up**.	Pick up your clothes, please. Sure. I'**ll** pick them up.

A Complete the requests with these words. Then compare with a partner.

| the books | the toys | the radio | your coat | the TV |

| your boots | the yard | the light | the trash | your cigarette |

1. Pick up .... *the toys* .... , please.
2. Turn .... off, please.
3. Clean .... up, please.
4. Please put .... away.
5. Please turn down ....

6. Please take off ....
7. Hang .... up, please.
8. Please take out ....
9. Please put .... out.
10. Turn on .... , please.

B *Pair work* Take turns making the requests above. Respond with pronouns.

A: Pick up the toys, please.
B: Sure. I'll pick them up.

4 PRONUNCIATION *Stress with two-part verbs*

A 🔊 Listen and practice. Both words in a two-part verb receive equal stress.

Please **túrn dówn** the radio.   **Túrn** it **dówn**.
Píck the magazines **úp**, please.   **Píck** them **úp**.

B Write four more requests using the verbs in Exercise 3.
Then practice with a partner. Pay attention to stress.

5 **WORD POWER** *Household chores*

A Find a phrase in the list that is usually paired with each verb. (Some phrases go with more than one verb.) Can you think of one more phrase for each verb?

| the counter | the cat | the dry cleaning | the faucet | the groceries |
| the mess | the oven | the garbage | the newspapers | the towels |

clean off	....	....	put out	....	....
clean up	....	....	take out	....	....
hang up	....	....	throw out	....	....
pick up	....	....	turn off	....	....
put away	....	....	turn on	....	....

B What requests can you make in each of these places? Write four requests and four unusual excuses. Use two-part verbs.

| the kitchen | the living room |
| the bathroom | the bedroom |

C *Pair work* Take turns making the requests you wrote in part B. Respond by giving an unusual excuse.

A: Mark, please clean up your mess in the kitchen.
B: I can't clean it up right now. I have to take the cat out for a walk.

6 **LISTENING** *Excuses, excuses!*

A 📀 Listen to parents ask their children to do things. Match each conversation with the picture it describes. Number the pictures from 1 to 5.

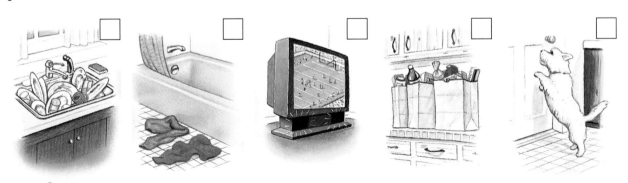

B 📀 Listen again. What excuse does each person give?

7 CONVERSATION

A 🎧 Listen and practice.

George: Hi. I'm your new neighbor, George Rivera. I live next door.

Stephanie: Oh, hi. I'm Stephanie Lee.

George: So, you just moved in? Do you need anything?

Stephanie: Not right now. But thanks.

George: Well, let me know if you do. Um, by the way, would you mind turning your stereo down? The walls are really thin, so the sound goes right through to my apartment.

Stephanie: Oh, I'm sorry! I didn't realize that. I'll make sure to keep the volume down. Oh, by the way, is there a good Italian restaurant in the neighborhood?

George: Yeah. There's a great one a couple of blocks from here. Try their lasagna. It's delicious!

B *Pair work* Has a situation like the one in part A ever happened to you? What did you do?

8 APOLOGIES

People apologize in different ways.
For example, if someone complains about the noise from your stereo, you can:

apologize and . . .	**give an excuse**	"I'm sorry. I didn't realize."
	admit a mistake	"I forgot I left it on."
	make an offer	"I'll turn it down right now."
	make a promise	"I'll make sure to keep the volume down."

People often apologize in more than one way. For example, in Exercise 7, Stephanie apologized, gave an excuse, and made a promise.

A *Class activity* How do people usually apologize in your country? What do you usually do when you apologize?

B 🎧 Listen to three people complaining. What are they complaining about? How does the other person apologize? (More than one answer is possible.)

Complaint	Type of apology			
	give an excuse	admit a mistake	make an offer	make a promise
1.	☐	☐	☐	☐
2.	☐	☐	☐	☐
3.	☐	☐	☐	☐

9 GRAMMAR FOCUS

Requests with modals and Would you mind . . . ?

Modal + simple form of verb	Would you mind . . . ? + gerund
Can you **turn** the stereo **down?**	**Would** you **mind turning** the stereo **down?**
Could you **leave** the door open, please?	**Would** you **mind not closing** the door, please?
Would you please **keep** the noise down?	**Would** you **mind keeping** the noise down?

A Match the requests with the appropriate responses.
Then compare with a partner and practice them.
(More than one answer may be possible.)

1. Could you lend me twenty dollars? ....
2. Would you mind picking up a sandwich for me? ....
3. Can you help me move into my new apartment tomorrow? ....
4. Would you mind not smoking here? ....
5. Would you please move your car? It's blocking my driveway. ....
6. Would you mind not talking so loud? ....

a. We're sorry. We'll talk more quietly.
b. Sorry. I'll do it right away.
c. Oh, I'm sorry. I didn't realize this was the non-smoking section.
d. Are you kidding? I'm totally broke!
e. I'm really sorry, but I'm busy.
f. Sure, no problem. I'd be glad to.

B *Pair work* Take turns making the requests in part A. This time give your own responses.

C *Class activity* Think of five unusual requests. Go around the class and make your requests. How many people accepted and how many refused?

"I'm totally broke!"

10 WRITING

A Write a letter to a "rich relative," asking him or her to lend you some money. Explain why you need it and when you will pay it back.

> Dear Uncle John,
>
> I'm planning to drive across the U.S. by car when I graduate.
> The only problem is, I can't afford to buy a car. Would you
> mind lending me $4,000 to help me buy one? I'll pay you
> back as soon as I get a job. . . .

That's no excuse!
How good are you
at apologizing?
Turn to page
IC-7.

B *Pair work* Exchange letters with a partner. Write a reply to your partner's request.

11 READING

Summer in the Country

How is summer in the country different for young people from summer in the city?

a Fresh Air Fund camp

"Before I came here," one child said, "I thought swimming was running through an open fire hydrant."

"Here" is a summer camp that's only an hour from New York City – but a world away. This camp and four others nearby are run by the Fresh Air Fund. Since 1877, the fund has helped poor children from New York City spend summers in the country. Each year, over ten thousand children, ages 6 to 18, participate in the program. Some stay at a camp; others live with a host family. The fund pays for all expenses.

The camps are for 8- to 15-year-olds. At camp, children can learn about the stars, see deer and cows and other animals, and go hiking, fishing, and of course, swimming. The children learn responsibility by helping out with chores like making beds and waiting on tables. They also learn a lot from counselors, who are often college students from around the United States and from other countries.

summer in New York City

Host families from thirteen states and Canada volunteer to have children spend the summer with them. Many of these families have their own children. The visiting children become part of the family. They go with the family on picnics, to the pool or beach, and on trips. The children are from 6 to 12 years old when they make their first visit, and most are invited back. Some of the children and families become friends for life.

A Read the article. Imagine you work for the Fresh Air Fund. A mother wants to send her child and calls to ask for information. How would you answer these questions?

1. Is the Fresh Air Fund program new?
2. Are the camps far from New York City?
3. What are some things children do at camp?
4. Does the Fresh Air Fund run only summer camps?
5. Can a 7-year-old go to camp?
6. Can a 7-year-old live with a host family?
7. What are some things children do with host families?
8. Can a child who lives with a host family go back for a second year?

B *Pair work* Talk about these questions. Give reasons for your answers.

1. If you were a child in New York City, would you rather go to a camp or live with a host family?
2. Would you like to be a counselor at a Fresh Air Fund camp?
3. How does the Fresh Air Fund benefit children? host families?

7 What's this for?

1 SNAPSHOT

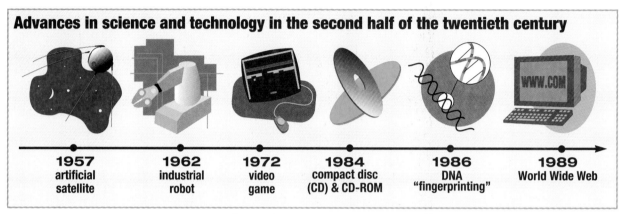

Advances in science and technology in the second half of the twentieth century

| 1957 artificial satellite | 1962 industrial robot | 1972 video game | 1984 compact disc (CD) & CD-ROM | 1986 DNA "fingerprinting" | 1989 World Wide Web |

Sources: *The Universal Almanac, The New York Public Library Source Desk Reference*

Talk about these questions.

*Can you explain the significance of each of these advances? Which
  do you think is the most important? the least important?*
Which have affected your life? Which have not?

2 CONVERSATION

A Listen and practice.

Daniel: Hey! Nice computer! What's this for?
Andrea: That's a modem. It's used to connect the
       computer to the phone line, so I can
       send faxes and access the Internet.
Daniel: So you can go on-line and all that?
Andrea: Yes. And I use the World Wide Web
       for finding information on astronomy,
       movies, UFOs – just about anything.
Daniel: Sports? Cars?
Andrea: Uh-huh. And I can exchange information
       with people, too. I belong to a "chat group"
       on astronomy.
Daniel: Hmm. I just use my computer to write
       letters and reports.
Andrea: Why don't you get on the Internet?
       It's not really expensive.
Daniel: Maybe I will. It sounds like fun.

B Listen to the rest of the conversation.
What else does Andrea use her computer for?

40

3 GRAMMAR FOCUS

Infinitives and gerunds

Infinitives and gerunds can describe a use or a purpose.

Infinitives	Gerunds
A modem is used **to connect** computers to phones.	It's used **for connecting** computers to phones.
Computers are often used **to write** letters.	They're often used **for writing** letters.
I can use the World Wide Web **to find** information.	I can use it **for finding** information.

A What do you know about this technology? Complete the phrases in column A with information from column B. Then compare with a partner. (More than one answer is possible.)

A

1. Satellites are used . . .
2. Robots are sometimes used . . .
3. You can use a fax machine . . .
4. People use the Internet . . .
5. DNA fingerprinting is used . . .
6. CD-ROM is sometimes used . . .

B

study the world's weather
perform dangerous tasks
read the latest weather
    report
transmit telephone calls
make a photocopy
identify criminals
make travel reservations
transmit television
    programs
store an encyclopedia

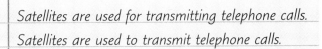

Satellites are used for transmitting telephone calls.

Satellites are used to transmit telephone calls.

B *Group work* Take turns completing the phrases in column A with your own information.

4 PRONUNCIATION Syllable stress

A Where is the stress in these words and compound nouns? Mark the stressed syllable. Then listen and check.

television programs	travel reservations	fingerprinting	fax machine
telephone calls	weather report	photocopy	Internet

B *Pair work* Practice the statements you wrote in Exercise 3. Pay attention to syllable stress.

5 WORD POWER The world of computers

A What are three uses for computers at home? at school? in a factory? in a restaurant? Complete the chart. Then add two more uses for each place.

communicate with people   create the menu   create work schedules
keep the attendance   make budgets   make report cards
pay household bills   pay the workers   place orders
process credit cards   research papers   run the machines

At home	At school	In a factory	In a restaurant
....	....	....	....
....	....	....	....
....	....	....	....
....	....	....	....
....	....	....	....

B *Group work* Compare your lists with classmates. Talk about the different uses for computers.

A: At home, people use computers to pay household bills.
B: My mother uses ours for making budgets.
C: I use mine to communicate with people on the Internet.

6 LISTENING

A *Pair work* How do you think these people use computers in their work? Make two guesses.

Sandy Watson is a police officer. She analyzes crime patterns.

Alex Hunt is a psychotherapist. He helps people change their behaviors.

Janet Brown is a professor. She teaches at a medical school.

....
....

B 🔊 Listen to interviews with the people in part A. Were your guesses correct?

7 CONVERSATION

A Listen and practice.

Jennifer: I read the instructions, but I'm still not sure how to use my cellular phone.

Richard: Actually, it's pretty easy. First of all, don't forget to turn it on.

Jennifer: Got it!

Richard: Then dial the number. And remember to press the "send" button.

Jennifer: That's all?

Richard: Pretty much. Just make sure to recharge the batteries every few weeks. And try not to drop it. It's fragile.

Jennifer: Good advice.

Richard: And one more thing: Be sure to pay the phone bill every month!

B *Class activity* How many advantages can you think of for owning a cellular phone?

8 GRAMMAR FOCUS

Infinitive complements

Don't forget to turn it on.
Remember to press the "send" button.
Make sure to recharge the batteries.
Try not to drop it.
Be sure to pay the phone bill every month.

A Look at these pieces of advice. Which ones refer to a microwave oven (**M**)? a hair dryer (**H**)? a laptop computer (**L**)? (More than one answer is possible.) Then think of another piece of advice for each thing.

1. Unplug it after you use it. ....
2. Save your work often. ....
3. Recharge the batteries often. ....
4. Keep it away from water. ....
5. Don't spill drinks on it. ....
6. Don't put metal in it. ....
7. Don't heat closed containers in it. ....
8. Don't expose it to extreme heat or cold. ....

B *Pair work* Take turns giving advice for using the items above. Use these phrases.

Don't forget to . . . .   Try to . . . .   Make sure to . . . .
Remember to . . . .   Try not to . . . .   Be sure not to . . . .

FREE ADVICE

A  Listen to people give advice about three of the things below. Write down the name of each item.

fax machine

motorbike

camcorder

in-line skates

ATM card

personal watercraft

	Item	Advice
1.	....	....
2.	....	....
3.	....	....

B  Listen again. Complete the chart with a piece of advice for each item. Then compare answers with classmates.

C *Group work* What do you know about the other items in the pictures? What advice would you give to someone about them?

"With a fax machine, remember to put the document facedown."

interchange 7

Good advice
Do you give good advice?
Student A turns to page
IC-9. Student B turns
to page IC-10.

 WRITING

Choose a useful item that you own. Imagine you're going to lend it to a friend. Write a paragraph giving advice on how to use it.

It's easy to use my fax machine. First, plug it into an electrical outlet. Then connect it to a phone line and turn it on. Remember to put the document facedown. Then dial the person's number. . . .

11 *READING*

A Day in Your Life – In the Year 2020

What are two ways that technology will probably change your life in the next 20–25 years?

People used to know more or less how their children would live. Now things are changing so quickly that we don't even know what our own lives will be like in a few years. What follows is not science fiction. It's how experts see the future.

You're daydreaming behind the wheel of your car, but that's OK. You have it on automatic pilot, and with its high-tech computers and cameras, your car "knows" how to get you home safely.

You're hungry, so you head for the kitchen as soon as you get home. You ordered groceries by computer an hour ago, and you know that by now they've arrived. Your kitchen has a two-way refrigerator, which opens to the outside to accept deliveries. You've already paid for the food by having the money subtracted from your bank account. Nobody uses cash anymore.

What's for lunch? In the old days, you used to stop off to buy a hamburger or pizza. Now you use your diagnostic machine to find out which foods your body needs. You find out you need more vegetables and less fat. Your food-preparation machine makes you a salad.

After lunch, you go down the hall to your home office. Here you have everything you need for doing your work. Thanks to your information screen and your new computer, you almost never go into the office anymore.

The information screen shows an urgent message from a co-worker in Brazil. You set the screen to translate Portuguese into English. As you wait, you think about later, when you'll have a movie transmitted. What movie should you order tonight?

A *Class activity* In your own words, tell about a change mentioned in the reading in each of these areas.

1. transportation
2. food
3. money
4. work
5. communications
6. entertainment

B *Pair work* Talk about these questions. Give reasons for your answers.

1. Which of the changes sounds the most interesting and useful? Are there any changes that you don't like?
2. Imagine you could invent a machine that would make life easier and better. Describe the machine.

8 Let's celebrate!

1 SNAPSHOT

Holidays and Festivals

Chinese New Year
January or February
Chinese people celebrate with firecrackers and lion dances.

Valentine's Day
February 14
People in many countries give chocolates, flowers, or jewelry to the person they love.

Children's Day (formerly Boys' Day)
May 5
Japanese families put up colored streamers shaped like fish, in honor of their children.

Day of the Dead
November 2
Mexican families offer food to the dead and then have a meal in a cemetery.

Thanksgiving
Fall
In October in Canada and in November in the United States, people celebrate the harvest by preparing a large meal. They usually serve roast turkey.

Source: *Reader's Digest Book of Facts*

Talk about these questions.

Do you have holidays similar to these in your country?
What other special days do you have? What's your favorite holiday or festival?

2 WORD POWER Celebrations

Pair work Complete the word map. Add two more words to each category.
Then compare with a partner

anniversary
cake
cards
champagne
dancing
fireworks
flowers
parade
party
presents
roast turkey
wedding

Special occasions
....
....
....
....

Activities
....
....
....
....

Celebrations

Special food and drink
....
....
....
....

Things we give/receive
....
....
....
....

3 *CONVERSATION*

A  Listen and practice.

Leo: Did you know next week is Halloween?
It's on October 31.
Natasha: So what do you do on Halloween?
We don't have that holiday in Russia.
Leo: Well, it's a day when kids dress up in
masks and costumes. They knock on
people's doors and ask for candy by
saying the words "Trick or treat!"
Natasha: Hmm. Sounds interesting.
Leo: But it's not just for kids. Lots of people have
costume parties. Hey . . . my friend Pete
is having a party. Would you like to go?
Natasha: Sure. I'd love to.

B Listen to the rest of the conversation. What are
Leo and Natasha going to wear to the Halloween party?

4 *GRAMMAR FOCUS*

> **Relative clauses of time**
>
> Halloween is **a day when kids in the United States dress up in masks and costumes.**
> November 2 is **the day when Mexicans observe the Day of the Dead.**
> Fall is **the season when people in the United States and Canada celebrate Thanksgiving.**

A How much do you know about these days and months? Complete the sentences
in column A with information from column B. Then compare with a partner.

A

1. New Year's Eve is a night when ....
2. April Fools' Day is a day when ....
3. May Day is a day when ....
4. Valentine's Day is a day when ....
5. July 14 is the day when ....
6. February is the month when ....

B

a. Brazilians celebrate Carnival.
b. people like to "party."
c. the French celebrate their revolution.
d. people play tricks on friends.
e. people in many countries honor workers.
f. people give presents to the ones they love.

B Complete these sentences with information of your own.
Then compare with a partner.

1. Winter is a season . . . .
2. Spring is a time of the year . . . .
3. Mother's Day is the day . . . .
4. A birthday is a day . . . .
5. A wedding anniversary is a time . . . .

5 LISTENING

Mike has just returned from Brazil.
Listen to him talk about Carnival.
Take notes to answer these questions.

What is Carnival?
How long does it last?
When is it?
What is the best part about it?
What is the samba?

Carnival in Brazil

6 ONCE A YEAR

A *Pair work* Take turns asking
and answering these questions
and others of your own.

What's the most interesting holiday
or festival in your country?
When is it?
How do people celebrate it?
Do you eat any special food?
What do you like most about it?
What else do people do?

B *Class activity* Give a short talk
about an interesting holiday or festival.
Answer any questions your
classmates may have.

Chinese New Year

Day of the Dead in Mexico

Children's Day in Japan

7 WRITING

A Write about your favorite holiday or festival.
What usually happens? What do you usually do?

> *My favorite holiday is Thanksgiving. In the United States, it's always the*
> *fourth Thursday in November. Everyone in my family gets together at my*
> *parents' house. We cook a large turkey and serve it with cranberry sauce. . . .*

B *Pair work* Read your partner's composition. Do you have any questions?

8 *CONVERSATION*

A 🔊 Listen and practice.

Jill: You look beautiful in that kimono, Mari. Is this your wedding photo?
Mari: Yes, it is.
Jill: Do most Japanese women wear kimonos when they get married?
Mari: Yes, many of them do. Then after the wedding ceremony, the bride usually changes into a Western bridal dress during the reception.
Jill: Oh, I didn't know that.

B 🔊 Listen to the rest of the conversation. Take notes to answer these questions.

Where was Mari's wedding held?
Who attended the wedding ceremony?
What happened at the reception?

9 *PRONUNCIATION* Stress and rhythm

A 🔊 Listen and practice. The words with the most important information in a sentence are usually stressed.

When **wóm**en get **már**ried in Jap**án**, they **úsu**ally **wéar** kim**ó**nos.
After the **wéd**ding **cér**emony, they **chánge** into **Wést**ern **clóthes**.

B 🔊 *Pair work* Mark the stress in these sentences. Listen and check. Then practice the sentences.

Halloween is a day when children go "trick-or-treating."
On Thanksgiving Day, Americans eat turkey and cranberry sauce.
When people have birthdays, they usually get presents from friends.
June is a month when many young people like to get married.

10 GRAMMAR FOCUS

Adverbial clauses of time

Before a Japanese couple gets married, they send wedding announcements.
When they get married, they usually wear kimonos.
After they return from the honeymoon, they move into their own home.

A Read this information about marriages in North America.
Match the clauses in column A with information from column B.

A

1. Before a man and a woman get married, ...
2. Before the man gets married, ...
3. When the woman gets engaged, ...
4. When the woman gets married, ...
5. After the couple gets married, ...
6. After they return from their honeymoon, ...

B

a. the newlyweds usually live on their own.
b. she usually wears a white wedding dress.
c. they usually date each other for a year or so.
d. his male friends often give him a bachelor party.
e. her female friends often give her a bridal shower.
f. there's usually a wedding reception.

B *Pair work* What happens when people get married in your country? Add your own information to the clauses in column A. Pay attention to rhythm and stress.

interchange 8

Once in a blue moon

How do your classmates celebrate special events? Turn to page IC-11.

11 MARRIAGE CUSTOMS

Group work Talk about marriage customs in your country. Ask these questions and others of your own.

How old are people usually when they get married?
Is there an engagement period? How long is it?
Who pays for the wedding?
Who is invited?
Where is the wedding ceremony usually held?
What happens during the ceremony?
What do the bride and groom usually wear?
Is there a reception after the ceremony?
What type of food is served at the reception?
What kinds of gifts do people usually give?
Where do couples like to go on their honeymoon?
How long is the honeymoon?

Mexico

Korea

Thailand

12 *READING*

Unique customs

Look at the photos below. What do you think is happening in each picture?

January 17 is **St. Anthony's Day** in Mexico. It's a day when people ask for protection for their animals. They bring their animals to church. But before the animals go into the church, the people usually dress them up in flowers and ribbons.

On August 15 of the lunar calendar, Koreans celebrate **Chusok** to give thanks for the new harvest. It's a day when people honor their ancestors by going to their graves to take them food and wine and clean the gravesites. Also on Chusok, a big meal with moon-shaped rice cakes is eaten.

One of the biggest celebrations in Argentina is **New Year's Eve**. On the evening of December 31, families get together and have a big meal. At midnight, fireworks explode everywhere and continue throughout the night. Friends and families meet for parties, which last until the next morning.

Long ago in India, a princess who needed help sent her silk bracelet to an emperor. After he helped the princess, the emperor kept the bracelet as a sign of the loyalty between them. Today in India, during the festival of **Rakhi**, men promise to be loyal to their women in exchange for a bracelet of silk, cotton, or gold thread.

On the evening of February 3, people in Japanese families take one dried bean for each year of their age and throw the beans around their homes and shrines, shouting "Good luck in! Evil spirits out!" This is known as **"Setsubun,"** a time to celebrate the end of winter and the beginning of spring.

A Read the article. Make five correct sentences using an item from each column.

A	B	C
On January 17,	people in Japan	visit the graves of their ancestors.
During Rakhi,	people in Argentina	bring their animals to church.
On Chusok,	men in India	stay up all night.
On New Year's Eve,	people in Mexico	celebrate the end of winter.
On February 3,	people in Korea	promise loyalty to their women.

B *Pair work* Is there a holiday or custom in your country that is similar to one described here? Describe the holiday or custom.

Review of Units 5–8

1 RESOLUTIONS

A *Group work* What are you planning to do or thinking about doing during the next year? Tell your group about at least three things.

"I'm going to take dancing lessons."
"I'll probably go on a diet."

B *Class activity* Tell the class about the most interesting or unusual plans in your group.

A: Bob is going to take dancing lessons.
B: And he thinks he'll go on a diet, too.

2 ON THE ROAD

A *Group work* Your friends are planning a long car trip for their next vacation. What plans do they need to make? How many suggestions can you think of? Use *had better, must, ought to, should,* and *shouldn't.*

A: You should take some road maps.
B: You'd better check the tires on your car.
C: You ought to check the oil.

B *Class activity* Compare your suggestions around the class.

3 ROLE PLAY *I'm sorry. I'll . . . .*

Student A: Complain to your partner about these things:

> Your partner has not returned your tennis racquet.
> Your partner is playing a CD loudly. You are trying to study.
> Your partner has been using the telephone for almost an hour. You need to make an important call.

Student B: Listen to your partner's complaints.
Apologize and make suitable responses.

Change roles and try the role play again.

4 WONDER GADGET

A *Group work* Imagine that this is a popular new gadget.
Think of as many possible uses for this item as you can.

A: You can use this gadget for . . . .
B: It's used to . . . .

B *Class activity* Tell the class your ideas.
Which uses do you think are the most interesting?

5 THAT'S AN INTERESTING CUSTOM.

A *Group work* What interesting customs do you know
for births, marriages, the seasons, or good luck? Take turns
talking about them like this:

"When a boy courts a girl in some parts of the Philippines,
he stands outside her house at night and sings to her."

Others ask questions.

Why does he do that?
Is it just a village custom?
Is it common?

B *Class activity* Which was the most interesting custom
you talked about in your group? Tell the class about it.

6 LISTENING

A 📟 Listen to some information about unusual marriage customs.
Check (✓) True or False for each statement.

Marriage customs	True	False
1. When two women of a tribe in Paraguay want to marry the same man, they put on boxing gloves and fight it out.	☐	☐
2. When a man and a woman get married in Malaysia, they eat cooked rice the day before the wedding.	☐	☐
3. In Italy, before a man and a woman get married, a friend or relative releases two white doves into the air.	☐	☐
4. In some parts of India, when a man and a woman get married, water is poured over them.	☐	☐

B 📟 Listen again. For the statements that you
marked false, write the correct information.

9 Back to the future

1 SNAPSHOT

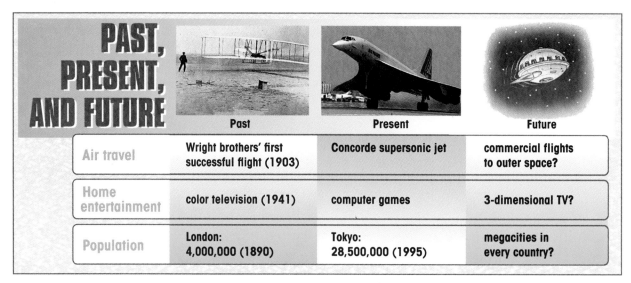

PAST, PRESENT, AND FUTURE	Past	Present	Future
Air travel	Wright brothers' first successful flight (1903)	Concorde supersonic jet	commercial flights to outer space?
Home entertainment	color television (1941)	computer games	3-dimensional TV?
Population	London: 4,000,000 (1890)	Tokyo: 28,500,000 (1995)	megacities in every country?

Source: *New York Public Library Book of Chronologies*

Talk about these questions.

Which of these past and present developments are the most important? Why?
Do you think any of the future developments will happen in your lifetime?
How will tomorrow's cities be different? Suggest three differences.

2 CONVERSATION

A 🔊 Listen and practice.

Mr. Lee: The neighborhood sure has changed!
  Karen: What was this place like before, Grandpa?
Mr. Lee: Well, there used to be a grocery store right here on this corner. Hmm. It was pretty quiet. Not many people lived here then.
  Karen: These days, the population is growing fast.
Mr. Lee: Yeah. I bet they'll tear down all these old buildings soon. In a few years, there will be just malls and high-rise apartments.
  Karen: Hey, that doesn't sound too bad!
Mr. Lee: No, but I'll miss the old days.

B *Class activity* How is your town or city changing?
List three important changes that are taking place.

54

3 GRAMMAR FOCUS

Time contrasts

Past	Present	Future
In the past, not many people **lived** here.	These days, the population **is growing** fast.	Soon, there **will be** a lot of high-rise apartments.
People **used to shop** at grocery stores.	Today, people **shop** at supermarkets.	In twenty years, people **might buy** groceries by computer.
Fifty years ago, people **lived** to around sixty.	Nowadays, people **live** to about seventy-five.	In the future, people **are going to live** even longer.

A Match the phrases in column A with the appropriate information from column B. Then compare with a partner.

A

1. Before the automobile, ...
2. Before there were supermarkets, ...
3. About five hundred years ago, ...
4. In most offices today, ...
5. In many cities nowadays, ...
6. Soon, ...
7. In the next hundred years, ...
8. Sometime in the future, ...

B

a. people used to shop at small stores.
b. pollution is becoming a serious problem.
c. most people are going to work at home.
d. people didn't travel as much from city to city.
e. there will probably be cities in space.
f. people work more than forty hours a week.
g. people played the first game of golf.
h. they might find a cure for the common cold.

B Complete these sentences with your own information. Then compare with a partner.

As a child, I used to . . . .   Next year, I'm going to . . . .
Five years ago, I . . . .   In ten years, I'll . . . .
Nowadays, I . . . .

4 PRONUNCIATION Intonation

A Listen and practice. Notice the intonation of these sentences.

Thirty years ago, very few people used computers.

Today, people use computers all the time.

In the future, there might be a computer in every home.

B Add your own information to the phrases in column A of Exercise 3. Read your statements to a partner. Pay attention to intonation.

5 LISTENING

Listen to people discuss changes. Check (✓) the topic each person talks about. What change has each person noticed? Are things better or worse than they were?

Topic		Change	Better	or	worse?
1. ☐ population	☐ environment	....	☐		☐
2. ☐ transportation	☐ cities	....	☐		☐
3. ☐ families	☐ shopping	....	☐		☐

6 CHANGING TIMES

Group work How have things changed? Choose two of these topics or topics of your own. Then choose a period of time and discuss the questions below.

Topics	
clothing	medicine
education	sports
entertainment	technology
housing	work

What was it like (fifty years ago)?
What is it like today?
What will it be like in (fifty years)?

Entertainment

A: Fifty years ago, there were very few TVs.
B: People used to listen to the radio.
C: Nowadays, ...

7 WRITING

A *Pair work* Interview your partner and write a paragraph about his or her hopes for the future. Don't write your partner's name on the paper.

> *In ten years, she'll be a successful actress. She'll be famous, and will star in movies and on TV. . . .*

B *Class activity* Pass your paragraphs around the class. Read one of the paragraphs. Can you guess who it is about?

8 *CONVERSATION*

A 🔊 Listen and practice.

Jody: Ugh! I feel awful. I really have to stop smoking.
Luis: So why don't you quit?
Jody: Well, if I quit, I might gain weight!
Luis: A lot of people do, but . . . .
Jody: And if I gain weight, I won't be able to fit into any of my clothes!
Luis: Well, you can always go on a diet.
Jody: Oh, no. I'm terrible at losing weight on diets. So if my clothes don't fit, I'll have to buy new ones. I'll have to get a part-time job, and . . . .
Luis: Listen, it *is* hard to quit, but it's not *that* hard. Do you want to know how I did it?

B 🔊 Listen to the rest of the conversation. What advice does Luis give Jody? How does Jody respond?

"I really have to stop smoking."

9 *GRAMMAR FOCUS*

> ### Conditional sentences with *if* clauses 🔊
>
> *Conditional sentences can describe situations and consequences that are possible in the present or future.*
>
> | Possible situation (with present tense forms) | Consequence (with future modals will, may, or might) |
> |---|---|
> | **If** I quit smoking, | I **might gain** weight. |
> | **If** I gain weight, | I **won't be able to* fit** into my clothes. |
> | **If** my clothes don't fit, | I'll **have to buy** new ones. |
> | **If** you get a part-time job, | you **may be able to* save** some money. |
>
> **Be able to is often used with other modals:* will *or* won't be able to, may be able to, might be able to.

A Match the clauses in column A with the appropriate information from column B. Then compare with a partner.

A

1. If you eat less sugar, ...
2. If you walk to work every day, ...
3. If you don't get enough sleep, ...
4. If you own a pet, ...
5. If you don't get married, ...

B

a. you may feel more relaxed.
b. you might feel healthier.
c. you'll stay in shape without joining a gym.
d. you'll have more money to spend on yourself.
e. you won't be able to stay awake in class.

B Add your own information to the clauses in column A. Then practice with a partner.

"If you eat less sugar, you'll lose weight."

10 WORD POWER Consequences

A *Pair work* Can you find two consequences for each possible event?
Complete the chart with information from the list.

be able to buy expensive clothes
feel better about yourself
feel hungry a lot
feel jealous sometimes
feel more energetic
feel safer in your home
have to give up your favorite snack
get requests for loans from friends
have to learn a new language
have to take it out for walks
lose touch with old friends
gain weight

Possible event	Consequences
buy a large dog	....
fall in love	....
go on a diet	....
inherit a lot of money	....
move to a foreign country	....
quit smoking	....

B *Group work* Can you think of one more consequence for each event?

11 UNEXPECTED CONSEQUENCES

interchange 9

Consider the consequences
Give your opinion about some issues. Turn to page IC-12.

A *Group work* Choose three possible events from Exercise 10.
One student completes an event with a consequence. The next
student adds a new consequence. Suggest at least five consequences.

A: If you buy a large dog, you'll have to take it out for walks every day.
B: If you take it out for walks every day, you might have an accident.
C: If you have an accident, you may have to go to the hospital.
D: If you go to the hospital, you won't be able to take care of your dog.
A: If you aren't able to take care of your dog, you'll probably have to sell it.

B *Class activity* Who has the most interesting consequences
for each event?

12 *READING*

Are You in Love?

What is the difference between "having a crush" on someone and falling in love?

You think you're falling in love. You're really attracted to a certain person. But this happened before, and it was just a "crush." How can you tell if it's real this time? Here's what our readers said:

If you're in love, . . .

♥ you'll find yourself talking to or telephoning the person for no reason. (You might pretend there's a reason, but often there's not.)

♥ you'll find yourself bringing this person into every conversation. ("When I was in Mexico – ," a friend begins. You interrupt with, "My boyfriend made a great Mexican dinner last week.")

♥ you might suddenly be interested in things you used to avoid. ("When a woman asks me to tell her all about football, I know she's fallen in love," said a TV sports announcer.)

OK, so you've fallen in love. But falling in love is one thing, and staying in love is another. How can you tell, as time passes, that you're still in love? If you stay in love, your relationship will change. You might not talk as much about the person you are in love with. You might not always call him or her so often. But this person will nevertheless become more and more important in your life.

You'll find that you can be yourself with this person. When you first fell in love, you were probably afraid to admit certain things about yourself. But now you can be totally honest. You can trust him or her to accept you just as you are. Falling in love is great – staying in love is even better!

A Read the article. What happens when you fall in love compared to when you stay in love? Check (✓) the correct boxes.

	Falling in love	Staying in love
1. You call the other person for no reason.	☐	☐
2. You can be honest about yourself.	☐	☐
3. You feel you can completely trust the other person.	☐	☐
4. You suddenly have new interests.	☐	☐
5. You talk about the other person at every opportunity.	☐	☐

B *Pair work* Talk about these questions.

1. The article lists several signs of being in love. Can you think of other signs?
2. Do you agree that staying in love is even better than falling in love? Is it more difficult?

I don't like working on weekends!

1 SNAPSHOT

The 10 Hottest Jobs in the United States

Expected number of new jobs, 1994–2005

Teacher	Nurse	Executive	Computer analyst	Truck driver	Social worker	Lawyer	Financial manager	Computer engineer	Accountant
606,000	473,000	466,000	445,000	271,000	187,000	183,000	182,000	177,000	120,000

Source: *Time* Magazine

Talk about these questions and complete the task.

Does any of this information surprise you? Why?

What jobs do you think are "hot" in your country? Are they the same as the jobs above?

Rank the jobs from the most interesting (1) to the least interesting (10).

2 CONVERSATION

A Listen and practice.

Brad: Any interesting jobs listed on the Internet today?

Sue: Well, there are a lot of retail jobs – selling clothes and stuff. But you have to work Saturdays and Sundays.

Brad: Hmm. I hate working on weekends.

Sue: Hmm . . . so do I. Oh, here's a job in sales. It's a job selling children's books to bookstores.

Brad: That sounds interesting.

Sue: Yeah. Let's see. You need to have a driver's license. And you have to work some evenings.

Brad: I don't mind working evenings during the week. And I enjoy driving. So, what's the phone number?

Sue: It's 798-3455.

B Listen to Brad call about the job. What else does the job require?

3 GRAMMAR FOCUS

Gerunds; short responses

Affirmative statements with gerunds	Agree	Disagree	Other verbs or phrases followed by gerunds
I like driving.	So do I.	Oh, I don't.	love
I hate working on weekends.	So do I.	Really? I like it.	enjoy
I'm good at using computers.	So am I.	Gee, I'm not.	be interested in

Negative statements with gerunds	Agree	Disagree
I don't mind working evenings.	Neither do I.	Well, I do.
I'm not good at writing reports.	Neither am I.	I am!
I can't stand making mistakes.	Neither can I.	Oh, I don't mind.

A *Pair work* Match the phrases in columns A and B to make statements about yourself. Then take turns reading your sentences and giving short responses.

A
1. I don't like ....
2. I'm not very good at ....
3. I'm good at ....
4. I hate ....
5. I can't stand ....
6. I'm interested in ....
7. I don't mind ....
8. I enjoy ....

B
a. talking on the phone.
b. working with a team.
c. solving problems.
d. sitting in meetings.
e. commuting to work.
f. making coffee for my boss.
g. organizing my time.
h. learning languages.

A: I don't like commuting to work.
B: Neither do I.

commuting to work in Tokyo

B *Group work* Write five more statements about yourself like the ones above. Then talk about your statements. Other students ask for more information.

A: I'm interested in working abroad.
B: Really? Where would you like to work?
A: Maybe in Mexico or Chile.

4 PRONUNCIATION Not, don't, *and* can't

A Listen and practice. Notice how the final *t* in **not, don't,** and **can't** is not released.

I'm no**t** good at filing and typing.
I don'**t** like doing sales work.
I can'**t** stand working from nine to five.

B *Pair work* Write three sentences using *don't like, can't stand,* and *not good at*. Then practice the sentences. Pay attention to the reduction of the **t**.

5 *LISTENING* Job hunting

A 📀 Listen to people talk about the kind of work they are looking for. Check (✓) the job that would be best for each person.

Best job		
1. ☐ flight attendant	2. ☐ lawyer	3. ☐ marine biologist
☐ teacher	☐ bookkeeper	☐ model
☐ songwriter	☐ doctor	☐ architect

B 📀 Listen again. What did each person say that made you choose the jobs you did?

6 *JOB PROFILE*

A *Group work* What are your skills and job preferences? Take turns asking questions like these and others of your own.

Are you good at . . .
   communicating with people?
   remembering names?
   solving problems?
   making decisions quickly?
   meeting deadlines?

Do you . . .
   have any special skills?
   have any experience?
   have any special certificates
     or diplomas?
   speak any foreign languages?

Do you like . . .
   traveling?
   commuting?
   working evenings?

A: Are you good at communicating with people, Juan?
B: Oh, sure. I enjoy talking to people. How about you, Su Hee?
C: Oh, I don't. I'm a little shy. What about you, Maria?
A: . . .

B *Group work* Prepare a personal job profile. Write down your name, skills, and job preferences. Then compare profiles with your classmates. Make suggestions for possible jobs.

"You like solving problems. So I think you should be an executive."

interchange 10

Dream job
Decide who to hire for a job. Student A turns to page IC-13. Student B turns to page IC-14.

7 WORD POWER Personality traits

A Are these adjectives positive or negative? Write **P** or **N** next to each word. Do you know any people with these personality traits?

bad-tempered	.....N.....	hardworking	....
creative	....	impatient	....
critical	....	level-headed	....
disorganized	....	moody	....
efficient	....	punctual	....
forgetful	....	reliable	....
generous	....	strict	....

bad-tempered

"My neighbor is bad-tempered . . . ."

B Listen to four conversations about these people. Check (✓) the adjective that best describes each person.

disorganized

Best description			
1. a boss	**2. a co-worker**	**3. a teacher**	**4. a relative**
☐ creative	☐ unfriendly	☐ moody	☐ bad-tempered
☐ forgetful	☐ generous	☐ patient	☐ disorganized
☐ serious	☐ strange	☐ hardworking	☐ reliable

8 CONVERSATION

A 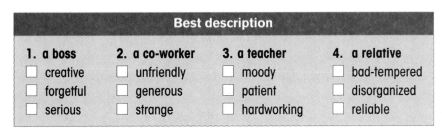 Listen and practice.

Tim: I don't know what classes to take this semester. I can't decide what I want to do with my life. Have you thought about it, Brenda?

Brenda: Yes, I have. I think I'd make a good journalist because I love writing.

Tim: Maybe I could be a teacher because I'm very creative. And I like working with kids.

Brenda: Oh, I wouldn't want to be a teacher. I'm too impatient.

Tim: I know one thing I could never do.

Brenda: What's that?

Tim: I could never be a stockbroker because I'm not good at making decisions quickly.

B Listen to Tim and Brenda discuss two more jobs. What are the jobs? Why wouldn't they be good at them?

9 GRAMMAR FOCUS

Clauses with because

Because *introduces a cause or reason.*
I'd make a good journalist **because I love writing.**
I wouldn't want to be a teacher **because I'm too impatient.**
I could be a teacher **because I'm very creative.**
I could never be a stockbroker **because I'm not good at making decisions quickly.**

A Complete the sentences in column A with appropriate information from column B. Then compare with a partner.

A

1. I wouldn't want to be an accountant ....
2. I'd like to be a novelist ....
3. I could never be a nurse ....
4. I would make a bad waiter ....
5. I could be a flight attendant ....

B

a. because I don't like hospitals.
b. because I really like traveling.
c. because I'm very forgetful.
d. because I'm terrible at math.
e. because I'm very creative.

B *Group work* Think about your personal qualities and skills. Then complete these statements. Take turns discussing them with your group.

I could never be a . . . because . . . .
I wouldn't mind working as a . . . because . . . .
I'd make a good . . . because . . . .

C *Class activity* Choose some statements made by members of your group. Share them with the rest of the class.

10 WRITING

A Write either about a job you would be good at or a job that you could never do. Give at least three reasons for your choice.

> *I think I'd make a good flight attendant because I'm*
> *a very friendly person and I enjoy meeting people.*
> *Also, I love to travel. . . .*

B *Pair work* Exchange papers. Do you agree with your partner? Why or why not?

"I think I'd make a good flight attendant."

11 READING

Find the Job That's Right for You!

How would you look for a job that's right for you?

the Artistic type at work

Nearly 50% of all workers have jobs they aren't happy with. Don't let this happen to you! If you want to find the right job, don't rush to look through the ads in the newspaper. Instead, sit down and think about yourself. What kind of person are you? What makes you happy?

According to psychologist John Holland, there are six types of personalities. Nobody is just one type, but most people are mainly one type. For each type, there are certain jobs that might be right and others that are probably wrong.

- The **Realistic** type is practical and likes working with machines and tools.
- The **Investigative** type is curious and likes to learn, analyze situations, and solve problems.
- The **Artistic** type is imaginative and likes to express himself/herself by creating art.
- The **Social** type is friendly and likes helping or training other people.
- The **Enterprising** type is outgoing and likes to persuade or lead other people.
- The **Conventional** type is careful and likes to follow routines and keep track of details.

If you think about who you are, *you can make the right job decision.* Liz is a good example. Liz knew she wanted to do something for children. She thought she could help children as a school counselor or a lawyer. She took counseling and law courses – and hated them. After talking to a career counselor, she realized the problem was that she's an Artistic type. Liz studied film, and she now produces children's TV shows – and loves it.

A Based on the information in the article, check (✓) the job you feel would *not* be a good choice for each personality type. Then explain your answers to a partner.

1. Artistic
- ☐ actor
- ☐ computer programmer
- ☐ photographer
- ☐ songwriter

2. Conventional
- ☐ accountant
- ☐ bookkeeper
- ☐ inventor
- ☐ secretary

3. Enterprising
- ☐ painter
- ☐ manager
- ☐ politician
- ☐ salesperson

4. Investigative
- ☐ detective
- ☐ model
- ☐ psychologist
- ☐ researcher

5. Realistic
- ☐ carpenter
- ☐ factory worker
- ☐ mechanic
- ☐ reporter

6. Social
- ☐ doctor
- ☐ nurse
- ☐ writer
- ☐ teacher

B *Pair work* Talk about these questions.

1. Which personality type are you most similar to? What kinds of jobs do you think would fit your personality?
2. Can you think of someone who has the wrong job for his or her personality? Explain why.

 **It's really worth seeing!**

1 SNAPSHOT

Famous Landmarks

The Great Wall of China was begun in 214 B.C. It is the largest structure ever built.

The Colosseum in Rome was opened in 80 A.D. It was sometimes filled with water for ship battles.

The Taj Mahal in India was built between 1630 and 1652. It is a tomb for the wife of an Indian prince.

The Statue of Liberty in New York was opened in 1886. It was a gift to Americans from the people of France.

The Eiffel Tower in Paris was completed in 1889. It was built for the 100th anniversary of the French Revolution.

Source: *World Book Encyclopedia*

Talk about these questions.

Have you ever seen any of these landmarks? Do you know anyone who has?

What else do you know about these places?

What are the three most famous landmarks in your country?

2 CONVERSATION Sightseeing

A Listen and practice.

Guide: We are now approaching the famous Statue of Liberty, which has welcomed visitors to New York Harbor since 1886.

Andrew: Wow! Look at it.

James: Incredible, isn't it?

Guide: The statue was given to the United States by the people of France. It was designed by the French sculptor Bartholdi.

Andrew: It's really huge. Do we get to go inside?

James: Of course. We can climb the stairs all the way up to the crown.

Andrew: Stairs? There's no elevator?

James: Not to the top. But it's just 142 steps!

B Listen to what else the guide says. What is the Statue of Liberty made of? How many people visit the statue every year?

66

3 GRAMMAR FOCUS

Passive with by (simple past) 🔊

The passive changes the focus of a sentence. For the simple past, use the past of be + past participle.

Active	Passive
Bartholdi **designed** the Statue of Liberty.	The Statue of Liberty **was designed by** Bartholdi.
The French **gave** the statue to the U.S. in 1886.	The statue **was given** to the U.S. **by** the French in 1886.

A Do you know who created these popular works? Match the phrases in column A with the appropriate information from column B. Then compare with a partner.

A

1. The *Mona Lisa* ....
2. The opera *La Bohème* ....
3. The novel *To Kill a Mockingbird* ....
4. The film *E.T. – The Extra-Terrestrial* ....
5. The album *Thriller* ....

B

a. was directed by Steven Spielberg.
b. was written by Harper Lee.
c. was recorded by Michael Jackson.
d. was composed by Giacomo Puccini.
e. was painted by Leonardo da Vinci.

B *Pair work* Change these sentences into passive sentences with *by*.
Then take turns reading them aloud.

1. Thomas Edison invented the phonograph in 1877.
2. Marie Curie discovered radium in 1898.
3. Gabriel García Márquez wrote *One Hundred Years of Solitude* in 1971.
4. Tim Berners-Lee developed the World Wide Web in 1989.
5. Woo Paik produced the first digital HDTV (high-definition television) in 1991.

4 TRUE OR FALSE?

A *Pair work* Write five statements like the ones in part A of Exercise 3.
Three statements should be true and two should be false.

B *Class activity* Read your statements to the class. Your classmates
say if they are true or false. They should give the correct information
for the false statements.

A: The cartoon character Mickey Mouse was created by Steven Spielberg.
B: False. Mickey Mouse was created by Walt Disney.

5 PRONUNCIATION Linked sounds

A 🔊 Listen and practice. Final consonant sounds are often linked to the vowel sounds that follow them.

The Colosseum‿in Rome was‿opened‿in 80 A.D.

The light bulb was‿invented by Thomas‿Edison.

B 🔊 Mark the linked sounds in these sentences. Listen and check. Then practice the sentences.

The Eiffel Tower was an important advance in engineering.

The Taj Mahal is a tomb for the wife of an Indian prince.

6 LISTENING Ancient monuments

🔊 Listen to three tour guides describe some very old monuments. Take notes to answer the questions below. Then compare with a partner.

the Pyramids

Machu Picchu

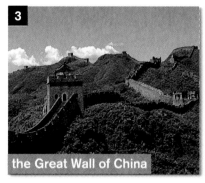
the Great Wall of China

Who built them?
Why were they built?

When was it begun?
When was it discovered?

Why was it built?
How long is it?

7 WORD POWER Features of countries

A Complete the chart with words from the list.

beef
Buddhists
mining
peso
Christians
Muslims

dollar
electronics
tourism
cheese
pound
wheat

Currencies	Religious groups	Industries	Agricultural products
....	....	....	....
....	....	....	....
....	....	....	....

B *Pair work* Think of a country for each of the items listed above.

"There are many Muslims in Indonesia."   "France produces cheese."

8 CONVERSATION

A 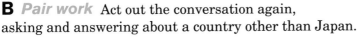 Listen and practice.

Linda: Hello?
John: Oh, hello. I need some information.
What currency is used in Japan?
Linda: Where?
John: In Japan.
Linda: I'm not sure. Isn't it the yen?
John: Oh, yes. And do they drive on the left or the right?
Linda: I think the left, but I'm not sure.
John: Oh. Well, is English spoken much there?
Linda: I really have no idea.
John: Huh? Well, what about credit cards? Are American Express cards accepted there?
Linda: How would I know?
John: Well, you're a travel agent, aren't you?
Linda: What? A travel agent? This is Linda's Hair Salon.
John: Oh, sorry. Wrong number!

B *Pair work* Act out the conversation again, asking and answering about a country other than Japan.

9 GRAMMAR FOCUS

Passive without *by* (simple present)

Active	Passive
They **use** the yen in Japan.	The yen **is used** in Japan.
They **speak** both Spanish and Portuguese in Latin America.	Both Spanish and Portuguese **are spoken** in Latin America.
They **grow** a lot of coffee in Brazil.	A lot of coffee **is grown** in Brazil.

A Complete the sentences. Use the passive of these verbs.

eat   grow   make up   manufacture   speak   teach   use   wear

1. Both French and English .... in Canada.
2. English .... in elementary school in Singapore.
3. A great deal of wheat .... in Russia.
4. Both cars and computers .... in South Korea.
5. Mexico .... of 31 states and a federal district.
6. Kimonos .... sometimes .... in Japan.
7. The baht is the currency that .... in Thailand.
8. A lot of beef .... in Argentina.

B Use the passive of the verbs in part A to write sentences about your country. Then compare with a partner.

69

10 WHAT DO YOU KNOW?

A *Pair work* How many of these questions can you answer?
See the appendix for the answers.

1. Where is Ecuador located?
2. What languages are spoken in Singapore?
3. Where is most of the world's wheat produced?
4. How many countries can you name where English is spoken as a second language?
5. Can you name four countries where French is spoken?
6. Can you name three countries that are governed by a prime minister?

B *Class activity* Write three more world-knowledge questions like
the ones in part A. Then ask them around the class.

11 LISTENING

Listen to a short talk about Colombia.
Complete the chart.

Facts about Colombia	
Location	....
Population	....
Language	....
Religion	....
Industries	....
Agricultural products	....

a coffee field

Bogotá, Colombia

12 WRITING

A Make an information chart like the one in Exercise 11 about a country
you know. Then write a short composition about it, but don't include
the country's name.

> *This small country is located in Asia. It has a population of around 3,000,000.*
> *English, Malay, Chinese , and Tamil are spoken. The population is made up of*
> *Buddhists, Muslims, Taoists, Christians, and Hindus. . . .*

B *Group work* Exchange compositions. Guess the names of the countries.

13 *READING*

Seven Modern Wonders of the World

Do you recognize any of the sites in the pictures?

Panama Canal

The ancient Greeks spoke of the Seven Wonders of the World. Recently, some engineers came up with this list of the seven wonders of our modern world:

The **Panama Canal**, begun in the 1880s, wasn't finished until 1914. It joins the Atlantic and Pacific oceans. Engineers describe the canal as a victory of humans over geography: Workers dug huge amounts of land and tamed rivers.

For 40 years after it was completed in 1931, the **Empire State Building**, in New York City, was the tallest building in the world. Amazingly, this 102-story building was constructed in just 410 days.

The **Netherlands North Sea Protection Works** is another victory over geography. The Netherlands, which is below sea level, was often flooded by the North Sea and by rivers. Then, between 1927 and 1932, a dam was built to shut out the sea. Twenty years later, dams and canals were built to control the rivers.

The **Golden Gate Bridge**, completed in 1937, was also a challenge for workers: San Francisco Bay has very strong winds and rough waves. The Golden Gate is still the world's tallest bridge. It has enough steel to wrap around the world three times.

At 1,815 feet, the **CN Tower**, in Toronto, Canada, is one of the world's tallest free-standing buildings. Completed in 1976, the tower is used for TV and radio broadcasting.

The **Itaipú Dam**, completed in 1984, goes across the Paraná River at the Brazil–Paraguay border. It is the world's largest hydroelectric plant.

Completed in 1994, the **Channel Tunnel** joins France and England. The "Chunnel" is a remarkable convenience: Cars, buses, and trucks are all carried through the tunnel by train.

CN Tower

Itaipú Dam

A Read the article. Then cover it and try to name . . .

1. a structure that is the tallest of its kind.
2. two great victories over geography.
3. a structure that joins two bodies of water.
4. two structures that join two separate areas of land.
5. a structure constructed very quickly.
6. two structures that are in Europe.

B *Pair work* Talk about these questions.

1. Which of these wonders would you most like to see? Why?
2. What other kinds of things could be described as "modern wonders"?

interchange 11

Traveler's profile
What kind of traveler are you? Turn to page IC-15.

It's been a long time!

1 SNAPSHOT

Success Stories

Oprah Winfrey
Richest entertainer in the U.S.A. (worth almost $200 million)

Personal: Born January 29, 1954, in Mississippi

Education: B.A. in speech and performing arts from Tennessee State University

Accomplishments:
- At 19, was first African-American news anchor on WTVF-TV in Nashville.
- Began *The Oprah Winfrey Show*, one of the most popular talk shows in the United States.
- After several years, formed a company and bought her own show!

William Henry Gates III
Richest businessman in the world (worth almost $20 billion)

Personal: Born October 28, 1955, in Seattle, Washington

Education: Dropped out of Harvard University after second year

Accomplishments:
- Wrote the first computer language for personal computers.
- At 19, founded Microsoft Corporation, the world's leading computer software company.
- At 31, became the world's youngest billionaire!

Sources: *The African-American Almanac, Forbes*

Talk about these questions.

What is the most impressive accomplishment of each of these people?

Name three successful people from your country. What have they accomplished?

2 CONVERSATION

A Listen and practice.

Richard: How did you get into modeling, Stacy?

Stacy: Well, when I graduated from drama school, I moved to Los Angeles to look for work as an actress. I was going to auditions every day, but I never got any parts. And I was running out of money.

Richard: So, what did you do?

Stacy: I got a job as a waitress in a seafood restaurant. While I was working there, a customer offered me some work as a model. Within a few weeks, I was modeling full time.

Richard: Wow, what a lucky break!

B  Listen to the rest of the conversation. What did Richard do after he graduated? What does he do now?

72

3 GRAMMAR FOCUS

Past continuous vs. simple past 🔊

Past continuous: for an action in progress in the past
I **was going** to auditions every day,
I **was running** out of money,
While I **was working** at the restaurant,

Simple past: for a completed action
but I never **got** any parts.
when I **got** a job as a waitress.
a customer **offered** me a job as a model.

A Complete these sentences. Then compare with a partner.

1. I .... (drive) in England when I suddenly .... (realize) I was on the wrong side of the road.
2. I .... (live) with my grandparents when I .... (enter) high school.
3. I .... (make) dinner last night when the phone .... (ring).
4. Tracy and Eric .... (work) in a restaurant in Vancouver when they .... (meet).
5. Several years ago, I .... (have) problems with math, so I .... (have) to find a tutor.
6. We .... (live) in a tiny apartment when our first child .... (be) born.
7. My brother .... (ice-skate) when he .... (break) his arm.
8. I .... (watch) TV when the power .... (go) out.

B Complete these sentences with interesting information about yourself. Use the simple past or the past continuous.

1. During my childhood, ...
2. I met my best friend while . . . .
3. When I was going to elementary school, ...
4. Two years ago, ...
5. Last year, ...

C *Pair work* Take turns reading your sentences from part B. Then ask and answer follow-up questions.

A: During my childhood, my family was living in Chile.
B: Oh, really? What were they doing there?
A: My father was working for a mining company.
B: . . .

useful expressions

Oh, really? That's interesting.
Why were you/did you . . . ?
Wow! That's incredible!

4 *LISTENING* Lucky breaks

Listen to people talk about their professions. What professions are they in? How did they get their lucky breaks?

	Celia	Rodney	Victor
Profession	....	....	....
Lucky break	....	....	....

5 *WORD POWER* Human ages

A What age range can each of these words be used for?

kid	*1 – 12*	woman	....	boy	....
infant	....	young person	....	man	....
child	....	middle-aged person	....	young adult	....
adolescent	....	baby	....	elderly person	....
girl	....	teenager	....		

B *Pair work* Compare your ideas.

A: I think a kid is between the ages of 1 and 12.
B: I think a kid can be between 1 and 17.

C *Class activity* Compare information around the class.

6 *WRITING*

A Write a short biography of an interesting person in your family –
a grandparent, an aunt or uncle – or of someone else you know about.

> My grandmother was born in Poland, but she moved to Toronto in
> 1946 when she was a teenager. She met my grandfather in 1955
> when she was working in a department store. After that, ...

B *Pair work* Exchange papers. Answer any questions your partner may have.

7 CONVERSATION

A  Listen and practice.

Pete: Hey, Joan! I haven't seen you in ages.
What have you been doing lately?
Joan: Nothing exciting. I've been working two jobs for
the last six months.
Pete: How come?
Joan: I'm saving up money for a trip to Europe.
Pete: Well, I've only been *spending* money. I quit my job
to go to graduate school. I'm studying journalism.
Joan: Really? How long have you been doing that?
Pete: For two years. Luckily, I finish next month.
I'm almost out of money.

B Listen to two other people at the party.
What has happened since they last saw each other?

8 GRAMMAR FOCUS

Present perfect continuous

Use the present perfect continuous for actions that start in the past and continue into the present.

What **have** you **been doing** lately?
I**'ve been working** two jobs for the last six months.

Have you **been saving** money?
No, I **haven't been saving** any money. I**'ve been spending** it.

A Complete these conversations. Then practice them with a partner.

1. A: What .... you .... (do) these days?
   B: Well, I .... (spend) my free time
   at the beach.

2. A: .... you .... (work) part time this year?
   B: Yes, I have. I .... (work) at a shoe store
   on the weekends.

3. A: How .... you .... (feel) lately?
   B: Great! I .... (get) a lot of sleep, and I
   .... (eat) too much fat or sugar.

4. A: .... you .... (get) enough
   exercise lately?
   B: No, I haven't. I .... (go) to the gym
   often enough.

B *Pair work* Take turns asking the questions in
part A. Give your own information.

9 *PRONUNCIATION* *Contrastive stress*

A 🔊 Listen and practice. You can change the meaning of a sentence by stressing different words.

I've been studying **journalism**. (normal stress)

A: Has your brother been studying journalism?
B: No, **I've** been studying journalism.

A: Are you going to study journalism?
B: No, I've **been** studying journalism.

A: Have you been teaching journalism?
B: No, I've been **studying** journalism.

A: Have you been studying literature?
B: No, I've been studying **journalism**.

B *Pair work* Practice this conversation. Pay attention to contrastive stress.

A: Has it been a year since I last saw you?
B: No, it's been two years.
A: Have you been losing weight?
B: Well, actually, I've been gaining weight.
A: Oh, and have you been going to school?
B: No, I've been teaching school.

interchange 12

Life is like a game!
Play a board game.
Turn to page IC-16.

10 *REALLY? HOW INTERESTING!*

A *Group work* What interesting things can you find out about your classmates? Ask these questions and others of your own.

Have you been doing anything exciting recently?
Are you studying anything right now?
　　How long have you been studying it?
Have you met anyone interesting lately?
Who is your best friend? How did you meet?
Where were you living ten years ago? Did you
　　like it there? What do you remember about it?
Have you been saving up to buy anything special?
　　How long have you been saving up for it?

useful expressions
Really? I didn't know that!
Oh, I see.
Gee, I had no idea.
Wow! Tell me more.

B *Class activity* Tell the class the most interesting thing you learned about someone in your group.

"I've been going skydiving."

11 *READING*

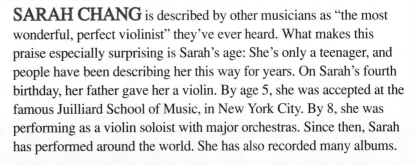

Child Prodigies

Do you know of any child prodigies?

SARAH CHANG is described by other musicians as "the most wonderful, perfect violinist" they've ever heard. What makes this praise especially surprising is Sarah's age: She's only a teenager, and people have been describing her this way for years. On Sarah's fourth birthday, her father gave her a violin. By age 5, she was accepted at the famous Juilliard School of Music, in New York City. By 8, she was performing as a violin soloist with major orchestras. Since then, Sarah has performed around the world. She has also recorded many albums.

Before **MICHAEL KEARNEY** was born, the doctors warned his parents that he might have learning difficulties. He's been proving them wrong ever since! By the time he was 4 months old, Michael could say full sentences like, "What's for dinner, Mom?" By 10 months, he could read words. Studying at home with his parents, Michael completed four grade levels each year. At 5, he entered high school – and finished in one year. By 10, he graduated from college with honors. At 11, he went to graduate school.

When **ALEXANDRA NECHITA** was 2, her parents gave her some crayons and coloring books. Alexandra was soon working in inks, watercolors, and by the time she was 7, oil paints. At 8, Alexandra had her first art exhibition. Her paintings are often compared to those of Picasso and other great artists. They have sold for as much as $80,000. She has been on TV, and a book of her paintings was published.

A Read the article. How did these three young people first show they were prodigies? What has each one accomplished? Complete the chart.

	When/How did he or she begin?	Accomplishment
Sarah	....	....
Michael	....	....
Alexandra	....	....

B *Pair work* Talk about these questions.

1. Which of the three prodigies do you think is the most amazing? Why?
2. If you were a prodigy, what would you like to be really good at? Why?

Review of Units 9–12

1 WHAT IF . . . ?

Pair work How will life change if these things happen?
Think of at least three possible consequences for each event.

If people stop watching television, ...
If people work only three days a week, ...
If people aren't allowed to drive cars in the city, ...

A: If people stop watching television, they might
read more books.
B: And they might spend more time with their friends.

2 ME, TOO!

Group work One student makes a statement about
one of these things.

Something you . . . .

are good at doing or not good at doing
can do well or can't do well
like or don't like
enjoy doing or don't enjoy doing
hate doing

Then that student says the name of someone else in
the group who responds and makes another statement.

A: I hate doing my laundry. *(says someone else's name)*
B: So do I! I can't whistle. *(says someone else's name)*
C: Neither can I.

3 WHO IS THIS BY?

A *Pair work* List ten novels, movies, songs, albums,
or other popular works.

B *Group work* Exchange lists with another pair. Take
turns saying a true statement about each item on the list.
Does everyone agree that each sentence is true?

"The novel *War and Peace* was written by Leo Tolstoy."
"The song 'Let It Be' was first sung by the Beatles."

novel: War and Peace
song: 'Let It Be'
movie: . . .

4 LISTENING

Listen to people on a TV game show answer questions about Spain. What are the answers? Complete the chart.

Facts about Spain

building in Barcelona by architect Gaudí

Currency	....
Driving	....
Population	....
Capital	....
Popular sport	....
Neighboring countries	....

Plaza Mayor, Madrid

5 MEMORY CHECK

Pair work Take turns asking and answering these questions.

What were you wearing . . . ?

yesterday
two days ago
on Saturday night

Who did you . . . ?

eat lunch with yesterday
talk to on the phone last night
last write a letter to?

6 TELL ME ABOUT IT

Group work Take turns asking these questions and four more of your own. Then ask for further information.

Have you been . . . lately?

working out
learning a new hobby
working long hours
taking driving lessons
reading any interesting books
doing anything unusual
traveling
dating someone new

A: Have you been working out lately?
B: Yes, I have. I've been going to a gym.
A: Really? What kind of exercise do you do there?
B: I usually take aerobics classes, but sometimes I swim.

13 A terrific book, but a terrible movie!

1 SNAPSHOT

Some of the world's most successful movies

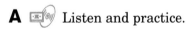

Movie	Year	Box office $ (in millions)
1. Star Wars	1977/1997	420.0
2. E.T. – The Extra-Terrestrial	1982	399.9
3. Jurassic Park	1993	356.5
4. Independence Day	1996	306.2
5. The Lion King	1994	300.4
6. Forrest Gump	1994	298.5
7. Home Alone	1990	285.8
8. Return of the Jedi	1983	263.7
9. Jaws	1975	260.0
10. Batman	1989	251.2

Source: *The Information Please Almanac*

Talk about these questions.

How many of these movies have you seen?
Which is your favorite? Why?
What are the three best movies you have seen in the last few years?

2 CONVERSATION

A 🎧 Listen and practice.

Paul: Do you want to see a movie tonight?
Carol: Hmm. Maybe. What's playing?
Lynn: How about the new Steven Spielberg film?
     I hear it's really exciting.
Carol: Who's Steven Spielberg?
Paul: You know. He directed *Jaws, E.T.*, and *Jurassic Park*.
Carol: Oh, *Jurassic Park* was boring. The book by Michael
     Crichton was fascinating, but the movie was terrible!
Lynn: Well, I'm interested in that new Johnny Depp movie.
     It's a romance. It's been playing for about a month.
Carol: Now that sounds good. I've never seen him in
     a romance, and I think he's a wonderful actor!

B 🎧 Listen to the rest of the conversation. What
happens next? What do they decide to do?

Johnny Depp

3 GRAMMAR FOCUS

Participles as adjectives

Present participles	Past participles
The new Johnny Depp movie sounds **interesting**.	I'm **interested** in the new Johnny Depp movie.
The movie *Jurassic Park* was **boring**.	I was **bored** by *Jurassic Park*.
The book was **fascinating**.	I was **fascinated** by the book.

Complete these sentences. Then compare with a partner.

Denzel Washington

Winona Ryder

1. Denzel Washington is a very .... actor. (interest)
2. I find nature films .... (fascinate)
3. I'm not .... in horror movies. (interest)
4. I'm .... with watching television. (bore)
5. I loved Winona Ryder's latest movie.
   I was .... that it didn't do better. (amaze)
6. I thought *Jurassic Park* was an .... book. (excite)
7. I'm .... by Michael Crichton's novels. (fascinate)
8. It's .... they don't make many
   westerns these days. (surprise)

4 WORD POWER Reactions

A Complete the chart with synonyms from the list.

absurd	dumb	marvelous	silly
bizarre	fabulous	odd	terrible
disgusting	fantastic	outstanding	unusual
dreadful	horrible	ridiculous	weird

awful	wonderful	stupid	strange
....	....	....	....
....	....	....	....
....	....	....	....
....	....	....	....

B Write six sentences like the ones in Exercise 3 about movies, actors, or novels.
Then compare with a partner. Does your partner agree?

5 LISTENING

Listen to people talk about books and movies. Check (✓)
the adjective that best describes what they say about each one.

1. ☐ fascinating	2. ☐ wonderful	3. ☐ boring	4. ☐ ridiculous
☐ silly	☐ odd	☐ terrific	☐ interesting
☐ strange	☐ boring	☐ dreadful	☐ exciting

6 PRONUNCIATION *Word and sentence stress*

A Which syllable is stressed in each of these words?
Mark the stress. Then listen and check. Practice the
words with a partner.

absurd	fantastic	outstanding	successful	terrible	unusual
amazing	fabulous	fascinating	ridiculous	surprising	terrific

B Listen and practice these sentences. Pay attention to stress.

It was a terrific book, but a terrible movie!
I thought *Jurassic Park* was ridiculous, but it was very successful.
Jaws was an exciting movie with many frightening scenes.

7 LET'S GO TO THE MOVIES!

A *Pair work* Take turns asking and answering
these questions and others of your own.

What kinds of movies are you interested in? Why?
What kinds of movies do you find boring?
Who are your favorite actors and actresses? Why?
Are there any actors you don't like?
What's one of the most exciting movies you
    have ever seen?
What did you like about it?
What are your three favorite movies in
    English? Why?
Are there any outstanding movies playing now?

A: What kinds of movies are you interested in?
B: I love action movies.
A: Really? Why is that?
B: They're exciting! What about you?
A: I think action movies are kind of silly. I prefer . . . .

B *Group work* Compare your information.

NOW SHOWING
on video

COMEDIES
THRILLERS
🎭 DRAMA 🎭
MYSTERIES
ACTION/ADVENTURE
SCIENCE FICTION
♥ *Romance* ♥ ♥
CLASSICS
DOCUMENTARIES
HORROR
ANIMATION

8 CONVERSATION

 Listen and practice.

Nina: This John Grisham novel looks interesting.
Alan: Oh, it is. It's about a guy who joins a corrupt
law firm and then can't leave. Luckily he has
a brave wife who helps him out of the mess.
Nina: Hmm. Maybe I'll read it.
Alan: Well, the movie is even better.
Nina: Oh, is that the movie that stars Tom Cruise?
Alan: Yeah. Why don't we rent the video?
Nina: You don't mind seeing it again?
Alan: Not at all. You rent the video, and I'll bring the popcorn.

a scene from the movie *The Firm*

9 GRAMMAR FOCUS

Relative clauses

Use **who** or **that** *for people.*	Use **which** or **that** *for things.*
It's about a guy. He joins a corrupt law firm.	It's a thriller. It stars Tom Cruise.
It's about a guy **who/that** joins a corrupt law firm.	It's a thriller **which/that** stars Tom Cruise.

A Rewrite B's answers using relative clauses. Then practice with a partner.

1. A: Have you heard of *West Side Story*?
   B: Yes, it's a musical. It has some wonderful songs.

2. A: What's the movie *Schindler's List* about?
   B: It's about an Austrian man. He saved the
   lives of many people during World War II.

3. A: Did you enjoy reading Stephen King's latest novel?
   B: Yes! It was a great book. It was hard to put down.

4. A: Who was George Gershwin?
   B: He was an American composer.
   He wrote lots of fantastic music.

5. A: Who is Steven Spielberg?
   B: He's a movie director. He's made some of
   the most successful movies of all time.

B *Pair work* Complete these sentences with relative
clauses. Then write three more sentences of your own.
Compare your information around the class.

1. Tom Cruise is an actor . . . .
2. *Star Wars* is a movie . . . .
3. Walt Disney was a famous movie director . . . .
4. Marilyn Monroe was an actress . . . .
5. *The Wizard of Oz* is a musical . . . .

West Side Story

The Wizard of Oz

10 SCRIPT WRITERS

A *Group work* You are script writers for a television studio. You have to write a new script for a TV detective show or mystery. Plan an interesting story. Make brief notes.

Where does the story take place?
Who are the main characters?
What are the main events?
How does the story end?

B *Class activity* Tell the class about your story.

"Our story is about two secret agents who are chasing after aliens from another planet. There are two main characters. . . ."

11 LISTENING

A Listen to two critics talk about a new movie. What do they like or not like about it? Rate each item in the chart from 1 to 3.

	Pauline	Colin
Acting	....	....
Story	....	....
Photography	....	....
Special effects	....	....

Ratings

1 = didn't like it
2 = OK
3 = liked it very much

B Look at the chart in part A. Guess how many stars each critic gave the movie. Then listen to the critics give their ratings.

★ poor   ★★ fair   ★★★ very good   ★★★★ excellent

interchange 13

At the movies
What do you know about movies and movie stars?
Turn to page IC-17.

12 WRITING *Movie reviews*

A *Pair work* Choose a movie you both have seen recently and discuss it. Then each person writes a review of it.

What was the movie about?
Did you enjoy it?
What did you like or not like about it?
How would you rate it?

B *Class activity* Read your review to the class. Who else has seen the movie? Do they agree with your review?

I recently saw . . . . It's a comedy that stars . . . . It's about a guy who gets lost in a large city. . . . The movie has good special effects and is very funny. . . . I give it . . . stars.

13 *READING*

Star Wars – Three Reviews

Have you ever seen the movie *Star Wars*?

Movie Director's Latest Triumph!

Don't believe people who say you can't improve a good thing. Director George Lucas has taken *Star Wars*, which was a hit back in 1977, and made it even better. There are new scenes, incredible special effects, and an improved soundtrack. But Lucas isn't just a technical genius. He also knows how to win our hearts. Everyone will love this science-fiction adventure story about growing up, friendship, and good against evil. Audiences will especially like the exciting chase scenes, shootouts, and Darth Vader, who is one of the greatest movie villains of all time. This movie is spectacular!

A New, Old Hit

Star Wars is back and better than ever . . . sort of. Yes, the soundtrack is clearer, but it's also louder. Yes, there are some new characters, but the old ones seem a little silly now. Even though it's a fun movie, and I liked it the first time I saw it, I expected this to be so much better. Maybe George Lucas should have made an entirely new movie.

"What Junk!"

Why did George Lucas spend his money and time on a tired old movie? There is a scene where Luke Skywalker, the hero, is rushing to the spaceship that will take him on his journey to save a princess, some robots, and, oh yes, the universe. When Luke sees the old spaceship, he exclaims, "What a piece of junk!" I knew exactly how he felt. This movie is just that, a piece of junk.

A Read the reviews. What rating would each critic give *Star Wars*? Circle the words in each review that helped you decide on the critics' ratings.

★ poor   ★★ fair   ★★★ very good   ★★★★ excellent

B *Pair work* Talk about these questions. Explain your answers.

1. Do you read movie reviews or watch movie critics on TV? Do they help you decide which movies you want to see?
2. What movie did you see when you were a child that is still special to you today?
3. What makes a movie great? terrible?

 **So that's what it means!**

1 SNAPSHOT

BODY LANGUAGE

Leave me alone!   That's finished.   I'm thinking.   I don't know.   I'm bored.

Source: *Bodytalk*

Talk about these questions.

Do people in your country use these gestures? Do you?
What other gestures do you use to communicate these meanings?
What are three other gestures you sometimes use? What do they mean?

2 CONVERSATION

A 🔊 Listen and practice.

   Ron: Have you met Raj, the student from India?
Laura: No, I haven't.
   Ron: Well, he seems really nice, but there's one thing
           I noticed. He moves his head from side to side
           when you talk to him. You know, like this.
Laura: Maybe it means he doesn't understand you.
   Ron: No, I don't think so.
Laura: Or it could mean he doesn't agree with you.
 Peter: Actually, people from India sometimes move
           their heads from side to side when they
           agree with what you're saying.
   Ron: Oh, so that's what it means!

B 🔊 Listen to Raj talking to his friend. What
does he find unusual about the way people in
North America communicate?

86

3 GRAMMAR FOCUS

Modals and adverbs

Modals	Adverbs
It **might/may** mean he doesn't understand you. It **could** mean he doesn't agree with you. It **must** mean he agrees with you.	**Maybe** it means he doesn't understand you. **Perhaps** it means he doesn't agree with you. That **probably** means he agrees with you.

A *Pair work* What do you think these gestures mean?
Make a statement about each gesture using the meanings
from the list. Then compare with a partner.

Gestures

Meanings

Hello!
Be quiet.
Peace.
We won!
That sounds crazy!
I can't hear you.
Come here.
Be careful.

A: What do you think number one means?
B: That probably means . . . . What do you think?
A: Yeah, or it could mean . . . .

B *Group work* Think of gestures that communicate these meanings.
Then take turns acting out your gestures. Can the group guess what
you are trying to communicate?

Go away.	Be quiet, please.	I'm angry!	I'm hungry.
I give up.	That's perfect!	I'm scared.	That's delicious.

4 WORD POWER Emotions

A What emotions do you think this person is communicating with his facial expressions? Match each picture with the emotion.

"He looks . . . ."

a. amazed
b. annoyed
c. confused
d. disgusted
e. embarrassed
f. excited
g. interested
h. shocked

B *Pair work* Take turns acting out the emotions above. Can you guess what your partner is trying to communicate? Use an *-ing* adjective.

"That's amazing!"

5 PLAY A GAME Charades

A Think of two other meanings that you can communicate with gestures or expressions. Write your meanings on slips of paper.

B *Class activity* Put all the papers in one pile. Each student takes two slips of paper. Take turns acting out the meanings. Can others in the class guess what you are trying to communicate?

A: Maybe that means . . . .
B: No, not exactly.
C: It might mean . . . .
B: Yes, that's close.

I'm tired of waiting.

6 PRONUNCIATION Emphatic stress

A Listen and practice. Words expressing strong emotions are often stressed and have higher pitch.

That was **amazing**!   You really **frightened** me!

B *Pair work* Write four sentences using these words. Then take turns reading your statements. Pay attention to emphatic stress in the sentences.

embarrassed   shocking   exciting   disgusted

7 PROVERBS

A *Group work* Here are some common proverbs in English. What do you think they mean?

A penny saved is a penny earned.
A stitch in time saves nine.
Don't burn your bridges behind you.

Every cloud has a silver lining.
One person's meat is another one's poison.
Don't count your chickens before they hatch.

"That could mean . . . ."

B Think of three interesting proverbs from your country.
Tell them to your group in English. What do they mean?

interchange 14

What's going on?
Interpret peoples' body
language. Turn to
page IC-18.

8 WRITING

A Write about one of your favorite proverbs. What does it mean? Why do you like it?

> *One of my favorite proverbs is "There are truths on one side of the mountain which are falsehoods on the other." I like this proverb because it states an important truth. What it means is that the things that some people think are true, other people may think are false.*

B *Class activity* Read your paragraph to the class.

9 CONVERSATION

A 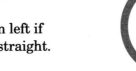 Listen and practice.

Vickie: You know, these highways are really great, but the road signs are pretty confusing.

John: Hmm. What do these lines on the road mean?

Vickie: They must mean you aren't allowed to pass here.

John: No. I don't think so. I'm going to pass this car in front of us. It's going too slow. Now, I wonder what that sign up ahead means.

Vickie: It may mean you've got to take a left in this lane.

John: Or maybe it means you can turn left if you want to. I think I'll just go straight.

B 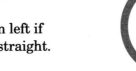 Listen to the rest of the conversation. Which picture shows the highway they were driving on? Which sign is the police officer talking about?

10 GRAMMAR FOCUS

Permission, obligation, and prohibition 🔊

Permission	Obligation	Prohibition
You **can** turn left here.	You **have to** turn left here.	You **can't** turn left here.
You**'re allowed to** pass here.	You**'ve got to** pass here.	You **aren't allowed to** pass here.

A What do you think these international signs mean? Match each sign with the correct meaning. Then compare with a partner.

1. .... 2. .... 3. .... 4. ....

5. .... 6. .... 7. .... 8. ....

Meanings

a. No playing ball.
b. Wear hard hats.
c. Swimming allowed.
d. Drinking water.
e. Do not touch.
f. Fasten seat belts.
g. No bicycles.
h. Recyclable.

B Write sentences about the meaning of each sign. Say where you might see each one. Then compare in groups.

Number one means you aren't allowed to touch something.
You might see this sign in a gift shop or a museum.

11 LISTENING *What's in a sign?*

A 🔊 Listen to people talk about the meaning of these signs. Number the signs they discuss from 1 to 5.

....

B *Group work* Draw a sign or symbol to express these meanings. Then compare with others. Who has the best sign or symbol for each one?

Remove your shoes.
Don't litter.

Children are allowed to enter.
You can't go off the path.

No dogs allowed.
Fishing is allowed.

12 **READING**

Body Language

What Does It Say?

What do you think is happening in the picture?

Kate   Lisa

More than half of what we communicate is communicated not through words but through body language. This includes our posture, facial expressions, and gestures. Because body language is so important, you'll want to know what yours is saying and how to interpret other people's, too. Here are some examples of body language and its meaning. (Note: These meanings are for North America. Interpretations may differ a bit in other cultures.)

If your posture is slumped and your head is down, this could mean that you are sad or lack confidence. If your posture is straight but relaxed, you are expressing confidence and friendliness.

A smile is a sign of friendliness and interest. But people sometimes smile just to be polite. To get another clue from people's faces, notice their eyes. Friendliness and interest are expressed when a person's eyes meet yours (especially when you're the one who's talking) and then look away and meet yours again. A person who doesn't look away is expressing a challenge. A person who doesn't look at you is expressing lack of interest or is shy.

Hand gestures can mean a person is interested in the conversation. But repeated movements – like tapping a pencil or tapping a foot – often mean the person is either impatient or nervous. Stay away from someone who points at you while talking with you: That person might be angry at you or feel superior to you.

A Read the article. Then circle the letter of the correct answer.

1. Look at the picture above. Who appears to be confident?

   a. Kate.   b. Lisa.   c. Both Kate and Lisa.

2. While you're talking to your boss, he or she is tapping a foot. This might be a sign that your boss:

   a. is impatient with what you're saying.   b. is interested in what you're saying.   c. feels he or she is superior to you.

3. If you want to show someone that you're interested, you should:

   a. continue to look at the person without stopping.   b. look away from the person.   c. look at the person but not for too long.

B *Pair work* Talk about these questions.

1. Do you agree with all the interpretations given in the article? If not, what don't you agree with?
2. How aware are you of people's body language?
3. What do you notice most – people's posture, facial expressions, or gestures?
4. Why do people sometimes express more through body language than through words?

15 What would you do?

1 SNAPSHOT

•Some stories of honesty•

Taxi Driver Returns Brazilian Soccer Player's World Cup Gold Medal and $60,000: is rewarded with $1,000 and souvenirs

Businessman tracks down owner of $750,000 and is thanked only with a phone call

STUDENT TURNS DETECTIVE to find owner of lost cash, credit cards, airline tickets, and jewelry; "I'm an honest man," the student tells relieved owner.

Homeless Mom and 3 Kids Return Lost $400 Check to Owner: Owner helps family move into house of their own

Source: *The Los Angeles Times*

Talk about these questions.

What would you do in these situations?

People who return lost things sometimes get a reward. Is that the meaning of the saying "Honesty pays"?

Have you ever found anything valuable? What did you do?

2 CONVERSATION

A 🎧 Listen and practice.

Lou: Look at this. Some guy found $750,000! He returned it and the owner thanked him with a phone call.

Kate: You're kidding! If I found $750,000, I wouldn't return it so fast.

Lou: Why? What would you do?

Kate: Well, I'd go straight to Las Vegas and try my luck in the casinos. I could double the money in a day and keep $750,000 for myself.

Lou: You might also lose it all in a day. And then you could go to jail.

Kate: Hmm. You've got a point there.

B 🎧 Listen to the rest of the conversation. What would Lou do if he found some money?

3 *GRAMMAR FOCUS*

Unreal conditional sentences with if clauses

Unreal conditional sentences describe imaginary situations and consequences in the present.

What **would** you **do if** you **found** $750,000?

Imaginary situation (*with simple past forms*)	*Imaginary consequence* (*with modals* would, might, *or* could)
If I found $750,000,	**I wouldn't return** it so fast.
	I might go to Las Vegas.
	I could double it in a casino.
	I would/I'd go straight to the police.

A Match the clauses in column A with information from column B. (More than one answer may be possible.) Then compare with a partner.

A

1. If I found a burglar in my home, ...
2. If I saw someone shoplifting, ...
3. If I found $75,000 on the street, ...
4. If the teacher gave me an A on a test by mistake, ...
5. If I locked myself out of my house, ...
6. If I won a million dollars in a lottery, ...

B

a. I'd break a window to get in.
b. I could think of ways to invest it.
c. I might not tell anybody.
d. I'd probably call the police.
e. I guess I might spend it.
f. I might tell a salesclerk.
g. I'd run to my neighbors for help.
h. I could get a set of keys from my friend.

B *Pair work* Add your own information to the clauses in column A. Then take turns reading your sentences aloud.

C *Group work* Think of three more situations like the ones in part A. Then ask another pair of students what they would do.

---

4 *LISTENING*

A 📼 Listen to three people talking about predicaments. Summarize each predicament and write it in the chart.

Predicament	Best suggestion
1.	....
2.	....
3.	....

B 📼 Listen again. What do you think the best suggestion was for each predicament? Complete the chart. Then compare answers with classmates.

5 PREDICAMENTS

A *Group work* What do you think you would do
or might do in these situations?

- you found a valuable piece of jewelry in a park
- you were on vacation overseas and lost all your money
  and credit cards
- you saw two people fighting in the street
- you discovered your friend has a drinking problem
- someone stole your clothes while you were swimming
  at the beach
- a friend borrowed money from you and didn't return it

A: What would you do if . . . ?
B: I'm not sure. I think I'd . . . .
C: I might . . . .

B *Class activity* Choose three of the best suggestions
and tell the class about them.

interchange 15

Do the right thing!
What would you do in
some difficult situations?
Turn to page IC-20.

6 WORD POWER Antonyms

A Find nine pairs of opposites in this list. Complete the chart.
Then compare with a partner.

enjoy	borrow	dislike	find	marry	lend
✓admit	remember	divorce	forget	refuse	save
agree	spend	accept	lose	✓deny	disagree

admit ≠ deny	≠	≠
≠	≠	≠
≠	≠	≠

B *Pair work* Choose four pairs of opposites. Write a sentence using each pair.

I can never save money because I spend it all on clothes.

94

7 CONVERSATION

A 🔊 Listen and practice.

Tanya: Is your houseguest still staying with you?
Ruth: No, after three weeks, she finally left. Thank goodness!
Tanya: So how did you get rid of her?
Ruth: Well, I lied and told her my parents were coming for a visit and I needed the room. I probably shouldn't have lied. Now I feel bad. What would you have done?
Tanya: Oh, I would have told her to leave after a week. By the way, my father-in-law is coming to visit us next week. Can I move in with you for a few days?
Ruth: No way!

B What would you do if a houseguest stayed too long?

8 GRAMMAR FOCUS

Past modals 🔊

Use would have *or* should have + *past participle to talk about imaginary or hypothetical actions in the past.*

What **would** you **have done**?	I **would have told** her to leave.
	I **wouldn't have done** anything.
What **should** I **have done**?	You **should have spoken** to her about it.
	You **shouldn't have lied** about it.

A Read the situations in column A. What would have been the best thing to do? Choose suggestions from column B. Then compare with a partner.

A

1. The teacher borrowed my favorite book and spilled coffee all over it. ....
2. I saw a classmate cheating on an exam. So I wrote her a letter about it. ....
3. A friend of mine always has messy hair. So I gave him a comb for his birthday. ....
4. I hit someone's car when I was leaving a parking lot. Luckily, no one saw me. ....
5. My aunt gave me a cigarette lighter for my birthday. But I don't smoke. So I gave it back to her. ....

B

a. You should have spoken to him about it.
b. I would have told her that I'd prefer something else.
c. I would have spoken to the teacher about it.
d. I would have waited for the owner to come back.
e. You should have exchanged it for something else.
f. I wouldn't have said anything.
g. You should have warned her not to do it again.
h. You should have left a note for the owner.

B *Group work* Make another suggestion for each situation above. Then compare answers with classmates.

9 PRONUNCIATION *Reduced form of* have

A 🔊 Listen and practice. Notice how **have** is reduced to /əv/ in the following sentences.

What would you **have** done?　　　　I would **have** told her to leave.

B *Pair work* Practice these sentences. Use the reduced form of **have.**

You shouldn't have lied.　　　　　　I would have said something.
You should have been honest.　　　　I wouldn't have said anything.

10 NO REGRETS

A Think about things that have happened in your life over the past few years. What opportunities did you miss? Write down five things you should or shouldn't have done.

> *I should have married my first girlfriend.*
> *I shouldn't have studied . . .*

B *Group work* Tell your classmates about your missed opportunities. Use the reduced form of **have**.

11 LISTENING

A 🔊 Listen to people calling Dr. Hilda, a counselor on a radio talk show. Complete the chart.

	What happened to the caller?	What did the caller do?	What should the caller have done?
Caller 1	....	....	....
Caller 2	....	....	....
Caller 3	....	....	....

B *Group work* Do you agree with Dr. Hilda? What would you have done?

12 READING

ask Alice

Do you read advice columns in newspapers and magazines?
Do you think they are helpful to everyone who reads them?

Dear Alice,

Someone told me that my brother's girlfriend was dating another guy. I felt I should let my brother know, and after I did, he confronted her with the story. Although she denied it, it caused a terrible argument and they almost broke up. Now it turns out that the rumor wasn't true, and my brother has stopped speaking to me.

Distraught Sister

Dear Alice,

I was at a friend's house for dinner recently. During dinner, I accidentally broke a beautiful vase. It was my friend's favorite wedding present. I offered to pay for it, but she refused. Should I have insisted? I still feel bad about it.

Feeling Guilty

Dear Alice,

My son is 23 years old. He finished college last year, but he can't seem to find a job that he likes. He still lives at home, and I'm worried that he's not trying hard enough to get a job and be on his own. Meanwhile, I've been cooking his meals and doing his laundry.

Tired Mom

Dear . . . ,

Well, you learned a lesson. You shouldn't have listened to gossip. And you shouldn't have passed it on. Now you have to repair the damage. Apologize sincerely and hope that he will forgive and forget.

Alice

Dear . . . ,

You're making it too easy for him to stay where he is. Be firm and tell him he has two months to find a job (any job) and get his own place. He's old enough to take care of himself – but you have to be willing to let him go.

Alice

Dear . . . ,

You should have thought more carefully before you acted. It wasn't necessary to get angry. Next time, speak to the child immediately and warn him or her not to do it again.

Alice

Dear . . . ,

I think you did the right thing. It was important to offer to pay for it, but it's not surprising that she refused. Perhaps you could give her a special gift to make up for it.

Alice

A Read the letters to the "Ask Alice" advice column and Alice's replies. Match the letters with the replies.

B *Pair work* Talk about these questions.

1. Do you agree with the advice in the letters? What advice would you give?
2. Think of a problem you or a friend is having. Ask your partner for advice.

13 WRITING

Write a letter to "Ask Alice" about a problem like the ones above. Then put your letters on the bulletin board. Choose one and write a reply to it.

16 What's your excuse?

1 SNAPSHOT

EXCUSES, EXCUSES

Situation	Excuse
Being late for an appointment	"My watch stopped." "The traffic was terrible!"
Forgetting an appointment	"I wrote the wrong date on my calendar." "I forgot to check my calendar."
Not doing homework	"My sister was using the computer." "I thought it was due tomorrow."
Getting home late	"I couldn't get a ride." "I missed the bus."
Not accepting a date	"I'm not allowed to date." "I have a boyfriend/girlfriend."

"I'm sorry I'm late. My watch stopped."

Talk about these questions.

Have you ever heard any of these excuses? Do you ever use any of them?
What other excuses might you give in these situations?
Do you think that you should always tell the truth?

2 CONVERSATION

 Listen and practice.

Daniel: Hi, Amanda.
Amanda: Oh, Daniel! I was going to call you tonight.
Daniel: What's up?
Amanda: Well, it's Albert's birthday on Saturday, and I'm planning a surprise party for him.
Daniel: Sounds like fun.
Amanda: The idea is this: I've asked Albert to go to a movie with me at six. After the movie, we go back to his apartment to have dinner. So be at Albert's by 7:30 to wait for us and surprise him. His roommate will let you in.
Daniel: OK. Great.
Amanda: Uh, can you bring some soda? Oh, and don't say anything to Albert.
Daniel: No problem.

98

3 GRAMMAR FOCUS

Reported speech: requests

Notice how requests are reported with the verbs ask, tell, *and* say + *the infinitive.*

Original request	Reported request
Can you bring some soda?	She **asked me to bring** some soda. She **told me to bring** some soda. She **said to bring** some soda.
Don't say anything to Albert.	She **asked me not to say** anything to Albert. She **told me not to say** anything to Albert. She **said not to say** anything to Albert.

Here are some things Amanda told the surprise-party guests. Write down her requests using *ask, tell,* or *say.* Then compare with a partner.

1. Meet at Albert's apartment at 7:30 on Saturday.
2. Can you bring your favorite CDs?
3. Don't bring any food.
4. Can you bring a small gift for Albert?
5. Don't spend more than $10 on the gift.
6. Be careful not to say anything about the party to him.

> *Amanda told them to meet*
> *at Albert's apartment at*
> *7:30 on Saturday.*

4 PICNIC AT THE PARK

A Imagine you're planning a picnic (or party). Write three positive and three negative requests for your guests.

> *Meet me at the park at 2 o'clock.*
> *Bring a baseball bat.*
> *Don't forget your bathing suit.*

B *Pair work* Take turns reading your requests. Confirm the information using reported requests.

A: You said to meet you at the park at 2 o'clock.
B: That's right.
A: You asked me to bring a baseball.
B: No, I asked you to bring a baseball bat.
A: Oh, that's right. And you told me . . . .

C *Group work* Join another pair and report what your partner told you.

"Charles is planning a picnic. He asked me to meet him at the park at 2 o'clock. . . ."

5 *WORD POWER* Collocation

A Find three words or phrases in the list that are usually paired with each verb.

anger   a compliment   a criticism   a joke   your regrets
an apology   a concern   an excuse   a lie   sympathy
a complaint   your congratulations   an invitation   a reason   the truth

express	....	....	....
give	....	....	....
make	....	....	....
offer	....	....	....
tell	....	....	....

B *Pair work* In what situations would you do the things in part A? Write five questions using the information in the chart. Then take turns asking and answering the questions.

A: When would you tell a lie?
B: Maybe if someone asked me how old I am.

6 *CONVERSATION*

A 🔊 Listen and practice.

Albert: Hi, Daniel. This is Albert.
Daniel: Oh, hi. How are things?
Albert: Just fine, thanks. Uh, are you doing anything on Saturday night?
Daniel: Hmm. Saturday night? Let me think. Oh, yes. My cousin just called to say he was flying in that night. I told him I would pick him up.
Albert: Oh, that's too bad! It's my birthday. I'm having dinner with Amanda, and I thought I'd invite more people and make it a party.
Daniel: Gee, I'm really sorry, but I won't be able to make it.
Albert: I'm sorry, too. But that's OK.

B *Pair work* Act out the conversation in part A. Make up your own excuse for not accepting Albert's invitation.

7 LISTENING

A  Listen to Albert inviting friends to his party on Saturday.
What excuses do people give for not coming? Match the person to the excuse.

1. Scott ....
2. Fumiko ....
3. Manuel ....
4. Regina ....

  a. She said that she wasn't feeling well.
  b. He said he was taking his mother to a dance club.
  c. She said she had houseguests for the weekend.
  d. He said that he would be out of town.
  e. She said she might go out with a friend.
  f. He said he was going away with his family.

B Listen. It's the night of Albert's birthday party.
What happens?

8 GRAMMAR FOCUS

Reported speech

If the reporting verb is in the past, the statement reported is usually changed to a form of the past.

Direct statement	Reported statement	
I'm **not feeling** well.	**She said** (that)	she **wasn't feeling** well.
There **is** an office party.		there **was** an office party.
I **visit** my mother every Saturday.		she **visited** her mother every Saturday.
I **made** a date with Jim.		she **had made** a date with Jim.
I **have planned** a trip		she **had planned** a trip.
I **can't come**.	He **told me** (that)	he **couldn't come**.
I **will be** out of town.		he **would be** out of town.
I **may go** out with a friend.		he **might go** out with a friend.

Cindy is having a party. Look at these excuses. Change them
into reported speech. Then compare with a partner.

1. Cindy: "There is a party on Saturday at my house."

> *Cindy said there was a party on Saturday at her house.*

2. Bob: "I'm leaving town for the weekend."
3. Mary: "I've been invited to a wedding on Saturday."
4. Jim: "I promised to help Joanne move."
5. Ann: "I can't come because I have the flu."
6. John: "I'll be studying for a test all weekend."
7. Susan: "I have to meet someone at the airport."
8. David: "I may have to work that night."

Please come to
a party at Cindy
Walker's home.

When:
Saturday, April 11.

Time:
7:00 P.M.

Why:
Just because!

9 PRONUNCIATION Had, would, *and* was

A 🔊 Listen to how **had**, **would**, and **was** are pronounced in these sentences.

She said she **had** forgotten the appointment.
He said he **would** be out of town.
She said she **was** busy.

B Practice the sentences you wrote in Exercise 8 again.
Pay attention to the pronunciation of **had**, **would**, and **was**.

10 NEVER ON SUNDAY!

A Your teacher wants to have an extra class on Sunday afternoon. You don't want to go. Make up an excuse.

> *I'm taking my dog to the hairdresser.*

B *Class activity* Talk to at least five classmates. What excuses do they give?

A: Are you coming to the class on Sunday?
B: No. I have an appointment with my psychic.

C Tell the class the best excuse you heard.

"Jack said he was taking his grandmother to a wrestling match."
"Sue said that she had a belly-dancing lesson."

11 LISTENING AND WRITING

🔊 Nancy is out of town for the weekend. Listen to four messages on her answering machine. Her roommate has written down the first one. Write down the other messages.

Nancy —   Friday, 9 P.M.
Bill called. He said he would meet you
in front of Pizza House at 6:30 P.M.
on Monday.

interchange 16

Excuses, excuses
Make plans with your partner. Student A turns to page IC-19. Student B turns to page IC-21.

12 READING

The Truth About Lying

MMMM... DELICIOUS!

Do you ever tell little lies? If yes, when and why?

It seems that everybody tells lies – well, not big lies, but what we call "white lies." Telling white lies isn't really that bad. Most of the time, people do it because they want to protect a friendship. Some studies suggest that the average person lies about seven times a day. The only real questions are about when we lie and who we tell lies to. A recent study found that people frequently stretch the truth. Here are some ways they do it.

#1 Lying to hide something:
People often lie because they want to hide something from someone. For example, a son doesn't tell his parents that he's dating a girl because he doesn't think they will like her. Instead, he says he's going out with the guys.

#2 Giving false excuses:
Sometimes people lie because they don't want to do something. For example, someone invites you to a party. You think it will be boring, so you say you're busy.

#3 Lying to make someone feel good:
Often we stretch the truth to make someone feel good. For example, your friend cooks dinner for you, but it tastes terrible. Do you say so? No! You probably say, "Mmm, this is delicious!"

#4 Lying to hide bad news:
Sometimes we don't want to tell someone bad news. For example, you have just had a very bad day at work, but you don't feel like talking about it. So if someone asks you about your day, you just say everything was fine.

A Read the article. Then look at these situations. Are they examples of 1, 2, 3, or 4? (More than one answer is possible.)

1. You borrowed a friend's motorcycle and scratched it. You're having it painted. When your friend wants the motorcycle back, you say the engine didn't sound right and you're having it checked. ....
2. Your friend gives you an ugly vase for your birthday. You say, "Oh, it's beautiful!" ....
3. You lost your job and are having trouble finding a new one. An old friend calls to find out how you are. You tell your friend you're busy writing a book. ....
4. Someone you don't like invites you to a movie, so you say, "I've already seen it." ....
5. You're planning a surprise party for a friend. To get her to come over at the right time, you ask her to stop by to see your new VCR. ....

B *Pair work* Talk about these questions.

1. Do you know of any other reasons people tell white lies?
2. When is it better to tell the truth rather than lie?
3. Do you ever give excuses that are not really true? When and why?

Review of Units 13-16

1 I SHOULDN'T HAVE . . . .

A Look at the five situations below and think about the past month. Then write down an example for each situation.

1. something you shouldn't have bought
2. someone you should have e-mailed or written to
3. someone you should have called
4. something you shouldn't have said
5. something you should have done

B *Pair work* Talk about each situation in part A.

A: I bought a lamp at a garage sale. I shouldn't have bought it because I really don't like it.
B: I did something similar recently. I shouldn't have bought . . . .

2 LISTENING

A Listen to some people talking. What are they talking about? Write down each topic below.

1. .... 2. .... 3. .... 4. ....

B Listen again. What does each person mean? Check (✓) the best response.

1. ☐ She is confused.
   ☐ She is afraid.

2. ☐ She enjoyed it.
   ☐ She hated it.

3. ☐ He couldn't understand it.
   ☐ He thought it was very interesting.

4. ☐ She thought it was all right.
   ☐ She thought it was terrible.

3 RULES AND REGULATIONS

A *Group work* How many rules can you think of for each of these places?

on an airplane	in an art museum	at a zoo
in a library	in a movie theater	in school

"On an airplane, you have to wear your seat belt when the plane is taking off and landing."

B *Class activity* Share your group's ideas.

useful expressions

You can/can't . . . .
You are/aren't allowed to . . . .
You have to . . . .

4 WHAT'S BEEN HAPPENING?

Group work Take turns asking and answering these questions.

Have you seen any frightening movies lately?
  Tell the group about it.
What is the most amusing show on TV these days?
  What is it about?
What is the most shocking news story you've read in
  the past year? Give some details.
Has a friend told you an amazing story recently?
  What was it about?
What is the most boring time you've had recently?
  Why were you so bored?

"I saw a movie about a person who . . . ."
"I find . . . amusing. It's about a family that . . . ."
"I was shocked by a story in the news last month. It was about . . . ."

a scene from the movie *Dracula*

5 THAT SOUNDS FANTASTIC!

A What would you do in these situations? Complete the chart.

If I had $1,000 to spend, ...
If I could invite anyone I wanted to dinner, ...
If I could take a vacation anywhere in the world, ...
If I could change one thing in the world, ...
If I could be a famous movie star, ...

B *Group work* Take turns comparing your answers.

6 GOOD INTENTIONS

A *Group work* What are some things you would like
to do in the near future? Think of three good intentions.

A: I'm going to try to learn how to sail.
B: That's interesting. Are you going to take lessons?
C: . . .

B *Class activity* Report the best intentions
you heard.

"Bob said he was going to try to learn how to sail"
"Terry told me that she wanted to spend more time studying."

Interchange Activities

interchange **1** **CLASS PROFILE**

A *Class activity* Go around the class and find out the information below. Then ask follow-up questions and take notes. Write a classmate's name only once.

"I used to look very different."

Find someone who . . .	Name	Notes
1. used to look very different.		
"Did you use to look very different?"		
2. used to have a favorite toy when he or she was a child.		
"Did you use to have a favorite toy when you were a child?"		
3. always listened to his or her teachers.		
"Did you always listen to your teachers?"		
4. hated high school.		
"Did you hate high school?"		
5. used to fight a lot with his or her brothers and sisters.		
"Did you use to fight a lot with your brothers and sisters?"		
6. dated someone for a long time in high school.		
"Did you "go steady" with someone in high school?"		
7. wanted to be a movie star when he or she was younger.		
"Did you want to be a movie star when you were younger?"		
8. had a pet when he or she was a child.		
"Did you have a pet when you were a child?"		

B *Group work* Tell the group the most interesting thing you learned about your classmates.

interchange **2** *MAKING THE CITY BETTER*

A Read this letter to a local newspaper.

Letters to the Editor

Dear Editor:

   I am sick and tired of the traffic in this city! It is so bad that I can never get anywhere on time. There are too many cars on the road, and most of them have only one person in them.

   Another problem is the buses. They are so old and slow that nobody wants to take them. They are noisy and very dirty. You can't even see out the windows!

   Also, the taxi drivers are rude. They never know where they are going, and they take a long time to get someplace. Taxis are expensive, too. And the subway is just too crowded and dangerous. What are we going to do?

                              George Grady
                              Oakville

B *Group work* Suggest five ways to solve the transportation problems in Oakville.

"Taxi drivers should take classes to learn how to be friendly."

C *Class activity* Tell your group's ideas to the class. Then decide which suggestions are best.

interchange 3 *WISHFUL THINKING*

A Complete this questionnaire with information about yourself.

WISH LIST

1. **What kind of vacation do you wish you could take?**
   I wish I ....
2. **What sport do you wish you could play?**
   ....
3. **Which country do you wish you could live in?**
   ....
4. **What kind of home do you wish you could have?**
   ....
5. **What kind of pet do you wish you could have?**
   ....
6. **What languages do you wish you could speak?**
   ....
7. **Which musical instrument do you wish you could play?**
   ....
8. **What kind of car do you wish you could buy?**
   ....
9. **What famous people do you wish you could meet?**
   ....
10. **What are two things you wish you could change about yourself?**
   ....

B *Pair work* Compare your questionnaires. Take turns asking and answering questions about your wishes.

A: What kind of vacation do you wish you could take?
B: I wish I could go on a safari.
A: Really? Why?
B: Well, I could take some great pictures of wild animals!

C *Class activity* Imagine that you are at a class reunion. It is ten years since you completed the questionnaire in part A. Tell the class about some wishes that have come true for your partner.

"Sue is a photographer now. She travels to Africa every year and takes pictures of wild animals. Her photos are in many magazines."

interchange 4 *RISKY BUSINESS*

A How much do you really know about your classmates?
Look at the survey and add two more situations to items 1 and 2.

	Name	Notes
1. Find someone who has . . .		
a. cried during a movie.	....	....
b. gone for a moonlight swim.	....	....
c. sung in a band.	....	....
d. studied all night for an exam.	....	....
e. lied about his or her age.	....	....
f.	....	....
g.	....	....
2. Find someone who has never . . .		
a. eaten a hot dog.	....	....
b. been on a blind date.	....	....
c. seen a wild animal.	....	....
d. kissed someone in public.	....	....
e. driven a car.	....	....
f.	....	....
g.	....	....

B *Class activity* Go around the class and ask the
questions in the survey. Write down the names of
classmates who answer "Yes" for item 1 and
"No" for item 2. Then ask follow-up questions
and take notes.

A: Have you ever cried during a movie?
B: Yes. I've cried during a lot of movies.
A: What kinds of movies?
B: Well, sad ones like *Casablanca* and . . . .

A: Have you ever eaten a hot dog?
C: No, I haven't
A: Why not?
C: Well, I'm a vegetarian.

C *Group work* Compare the
information in your surveys.

interchange 5 *FUN VACATIONS*

Student A

A *Pair work* You and your partner are going to take a trip. You have a brochure for a ski trip, and your partner has a brochure for a surfing trip. First ask questions like these about the surfing trip:

How much does the trip cost?
What does the price of the trip include?
What are the accommodations like?
Are surfing lessons available?
Is there going to be anything else to do? Tell me about the nightlife.
What else can you tell me about the trip?

B *Pair work* Now use the information in this brochure to answer your partner's questions about the ski trip.

Winter Wonderland USA

15-Day Ski Tour in the Green Mountains

Visit these ski resorts in Vermont:

**Killington • Okemo • Stowe
Stratton • Sugarbush**

Accommodations:	Country inns, with relaxing atmosphere and fine dining; luxurious rooms feature Jacuzzis and fireplaces
Price includes:	All ski equipment, lift tickets, and daily 2-hour lessons
Nightlife activities:	Candlelit dinners in the inn's restaurants, classical music concerts
Additional activities:	Go antique shopping, cross-country skiing, sledding, ice skating, horse-drawn sleigh rides
Tour cost:	Single room: $2,500 Double room: $3,200

C *Pair work* Decide which trip you are going to take. Then explain your choice to the class.

THAT'S NO EXCUSE!

A *Pair work* Look at these situations and act out conversations.
Apologize and then give an excuse, admit a mistake, make an offer, or
make a promise.

1

Student A: You're the customer.
Student B: You're the hairstylist.

A: My hair! You ruined my hair!
B: I'm so sorry. I . . . .

2

Student A: You own the puppy.
Student B: You own the backpack.

3

Student A: You're driving the red car.
Student B: You're driving the blue car.

4

Student A: You're the customer.
Student B: You're the cashier.

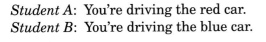

B *Group work* Have you ever experienced situations like these? What
happened? What did you do? Share your stories.

interchange 5 *FUN VACATIONS*

Student B

A *Pair work* You and your partner are going to take a trip. You have a brochure for a surfing trip, and your partner has a brochure for a ski trip. First, use the information in this brochure to answer your partner's questions about the surfing trip.

Summer Surfing USA

15-Day Tour for Beach Lovers

Visit these beautiful Southern California surfing beaches.
El Capitan in Santa Barbara, **Surf Riders** in Malibu,
The Wedge at Newport Beach, **Doheny** at Dana Point

Accommodations:	Single or double rooms in beachfront hotels
Price includes:	Daily surfboard rental, 3-hour beginner's class
Nightlife activities:	Beach barbecues, club dancing, moonlight cruise
Additional activities:	Visit Universal Studios and Disneyland
	Tour Beverly Hills and see the movie stars' homes
Tour cost:	Single room: $1,999
	Double room: $2,300

B *Pair work* Now ask questions like these about the ski trip:

How much does the trip cost?
What does the price of the trip include?
What are the accommodations like?
Are skiing lessons available?
Is there going to be anything else to do? Tell me
   about the nightlife.
What else can you tell me about the trip?

C *Pair work* Decide which trip you are going to take. Then explain your choice to the class.

interchange 7 *GOOD ADVICE*

Student A

A *Pair work* Ask your partner for advice about these situations.

> I'm going away on vacation and my house will be empty. How can I make my house safe from burglars?

> I'm buying a used car. How can I make sure that it's in good condition?

> I have an important job interview. How can I make a good impression?

A: I'm going away on vacation and my house will be empty.
How can I make my house safe from burglars?
B: Well, don't forget to lock all the windows. Oh, and make sure to . . . .

B *Pair work* Now your partner needs advice about these situations. Give at least four suggestions for each one.

useful expressions	
Don't forget to	Try not to . . . .
Remember to	Make sure to . . . .
Try to	Be sure not to . . . .

> Your partner is going to rent an apartment with a roommate.

> Your partner is meeting his girlfriend's or her boyfriend's parents for the first time.

> Your partner is mailing a valuable glass vase to a friend.

interchange 7 GOOD ADVICE

Student B

A *Pair work* Your partner needs advice about these situations. Give at least four suggestions for each one.

Your partner is going away on vacation and his or her house will be empty.

Your partner is buying a used car.

Your partner has an important job interview.

A: I'm going away on vacation and my house will be empty. How can I make my house safe from burglars?
B: Well, don't forget to lock all the windows. Oh, and make sure to . . . .

B *Pair work* Now ask your partner for advice about these situations.

I'm going to rent an apartment with a roommate. What can we do to get along well?

I'm meeting my girlfriend's/boyfriend's parents for the first time. How can I make a good impression?

I'm mailing a valuable glass vase to my friend. How can I make sure it arrives safely?

interchange 8 *ONCE IN A BLUE MOON*

A *Class activity* How do your classmates celebrate special days and times? Go around the class and ask the questions below. If someone answers "Yes," write down his or her name. Ask for more information and take notes.

A: Does your family have big get-togethers?
B: Yes, we do.
A: What do you do when you get together?
B: Well, we have a big meal. After we eat, we watch old home movies.

	Name	Notes
1. Does your family have big get-togethers?		
2. Do you ever buy flowers for someone special?		
3. Do you often take friends out to dinner?		
4. Do you wear your national dress at least once a year?		
5. Has someone given you money recently as a gift?		
6. Have you given money to someone recently as a gift?		
7. Do you like to celebrate your birthday with a party?		
8. Do you ever send birthday cards?		
9. Do you ever give friends birthday presents?		
10. Do you think long engagements are a good idea?		
11. Do you drink champagne at special events?		
12. Is New Year's your favorite time of the year?		
13. Do you ever celebrate a holiday with fireworks?		

B *Pair work* Compare your information with a partner.

interchange 9 **CONSIDER THE CONSEQUENCES**

A Read over this questionnaire. Check (✓) the column that states your opinion.

	I agree.	I don't agree.	It depends.
1. If they raise the price of cigarettes a lot, people will stop smoking.	☐	☐	☐
2. If the price of gas goes up a lot, people will drive less.	☐	☐	☐
3. If people work only four days a week, their lives will be better.	☐	☐	☐
4. If people have smaller families, they will have better lives.	☐	☐	☐
5. If women do not work outside the home, their children will be happier.	☐	☐	☐
6. If a woman becomes the leader of this country, a lot of things will change for the better.	☐	☐	☐
7. If children watch a lot of violent programs on TV, they will become violent themselves.	☐	☐	☐
8. If people watch less TV, they will spend more time with their families.	☐	☐	☐
9. If teachers do not give tests, students will not study.	☐	☐	☐

B *Group work* Compare your opinions. Be prepared to give reasons for your opinions.

A: I think that if they raise the price of cigarettes a lot, people will stop smoking.
B: I don't really agree.
C: Why not?
B: Well, it's very difficult for people to stop smoking.
A: But if you don't have much money, you may not be able to afford expensive cigarettes.

interchange 10 DREAM JOB

Student A

A *Pair work* You and your partner are co-owners of NIKO Sneakers, a large company that makes running and walking shoes. You are both looking for someone to be a marketing assistant. You interviewed Lynette Liu. First, read the job description. Then look at what Ms. Liu said during the interview and answer your partner's questions about her.

Marketing Assistant

Requirements:
- Must have a business degree or marketing experience
- Must be a "people person"
- Must enjoy sports and fitness activities – especially running and walking
- Must be available to work long hours
- Must be willing to travel

Responsibilities:
- Interviewing customers about their shoe preferences
- Writing reports about the customer interviews
- Working with famous athletes

niko sneakers

B *Pair work* Your partner interviewed James Marino. Ask questions like these to get information about him.

What kind of work experience does he have?
What kind of degree does he have?
Does he like meeting people?
Is he good at writing reports?

What kind of sports interest him?
Does he mind traveling?
Can he work long hours?
What else do you know about him?

C *Pair work* Work with your partner to decide who to hire for the job of marketing assistant, Lynette Liu or James Marino.

interchange 10 DREAM JOB

Student B

A *Pair work* You and your partner are co-owners of NIKO Sneakers, a large company that makes running and walking shoes. You are both looking for someone to be a marketing assistant. Your partner interviewed Lynette Liu. First, read the job description. Then ask questions like these to get information about her.

Marketing Assistant

Requirements:
- Must have a business degree or marketing experience
- Must be a "people person"
- Must enjoy sports and fitness activities – especially running and walking
- Must be available to work long hours
- Must be willing to travel

Responsibilities:
- Interviewing customers about their shoe preferences
- Writing reports about the customer interviews
- Working with famous athletes

niko sneakers

What kind of work experience does she have?
What kind of degree does she have?
Does she like meeting people?
Is she good at writing reports?

What kind of sports interest her?
Does she mind traveling?
Can she work long hours?
What else do you know about her?

B *Pair work* You interviewed James Marino. First, look at what he said during the interview. Then answer your partner's questions about him.

C *Pair work* Work with your partner to decide who to hire for the job of marketing assistant, Lynette Liu or James Marino.

interchange 11 *TRAVELER'S PROFILE*

A *Pair work* What kind of traveler are you (or do you think you would be)? Look at the three types of travelers. Which one is most like you? Why?

The "Just-In-Case" Traveler   The "Less-Is-Best" Traveler   The Invisible Traveler

B *Group work* Decide together which traveler each of these statements best describes. Check (✓) the appropriate column.

	The "Just-In-Case" Traveler	The "Less-Is-Best" Traveler	The Invisible Traveler
When this person travels, . . .			
1. the suitcase is packed days in advance.	☐	☐	☐
2. a bag is packed at the last minute.	☐	☐	☐
3. airplane tickets are bought months ahead.	☐	☐	☐
4. hotel rooms are usually not reserved.	☐	☐	☐
5. postcards are sent to every friend and relative.	☐	☐	☐
6. no money is spent on souvenirs.	☐	☐	☐
7. meals are often eaten at expensive restaurants.	☐	☐	☐
8. every minute of the trip is organized.	☐	☐	☐
9. a lot of photographs are taken.	☐	☐	☐

C *Class activity* Take a survey to find out which kind of travelers are in your class. Are most students "Just-In-Case" Travelers?

A: What kind of traveler are you, Rita?
B: Oh, I'm a "Just-In-Case" traveler. I always pack too many clothes when I go on vacation.
A: How about you, Michael?
C: . . .

interchange 12 *LIFE IS LIKE A GAME!*

A *Group work* Play the board game. Follow these instructions.

1. Use small pieces of paper with your initials on them as markers.

2. Take turns by tossing a coin:
   If the coin lands face up, move two spaces.
   If one coin lands face down, move one space.

3. Complete the sentence in the space you land on. Others ask two
   follow-up questions to get more information.

A: It's been a year since I started working.
B: Oh, really? Do you like your job?
A: Well, the job's just okay, but the money is great!
C: What do you do?
A: . . .

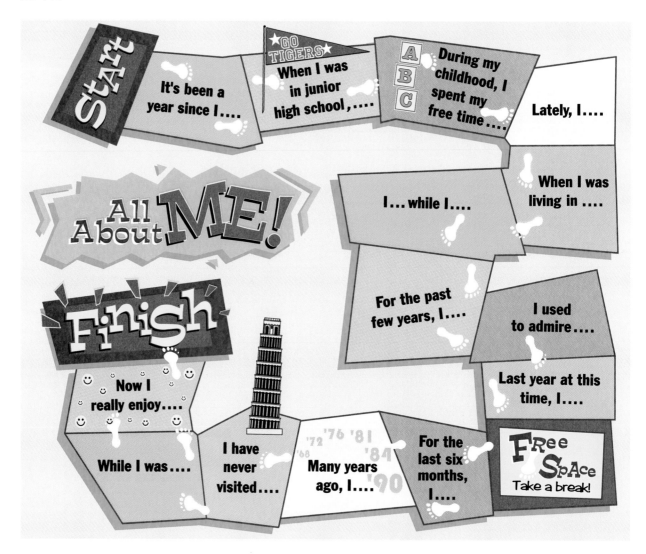

B *Class activity* Tell the class an interesting fact that you learned
about someone in your group.

"Last year at this time, Daniel was hiking in the Swiss Alps!"

interchange 13   *AT THE MOVIES*

A Complete this questionnaire.

What is the name of an actor or actress . . .
1. that reminds you of someone in your family? ....
2. that has beautiful eyes? ....
3. who does things to help society? ....
4. who has a beautiful speaking voice? ....
5. who isn't good-looking but who is very talented? ....
What is the name of a movie . . .
6. that made you feel sad? ....
7. that made you laugh a lot? ....
8. which scared you? ....
9. which had great music? ....
10. that was about a ridiculous story? ....

B *Pair work* Compare your questionnaires. Ask follow-up questions of your own.

A: What is the name of an actor or actress that reminds you of someone in your family?
B: Tom Cruise.
A: Who does he remind you of?
B: My brother, Todd.
A: Really? Why?
B: Because he looks like my brother. They have the same smile.

interchange **14** **WHAT'S GOING ON?**

A *Pair work* Look at this scene of a crowded restaurant. What do you think is happening in each of the five situations? Look at people's body language for clues.

A: Why do you think the woman in situation 1 looks upset?
B: Well, she might be having a fight with . . . .

A: What do you think the woman's gesture in situation 5 means?
B: Maybe it means she . . . .

B *Group work* Compare your interpretations. Do you agree or disagree?

interchange 16 EXCUSES, EXCUSES

Student A

A *Role play* You and your partner want to get together one evening in July. However, you are very busy and you also want to keep time open for other friends. You don't want to hurt your partner's feelings, so you make up excuses for many of the days in that month. Look at your calendar of evening plans. Then ask and answer questions to find out when you are both free. (Write your partner's excuses on the calendar.) Don't give up until you make a date.

A: Do you want to go out on the second?
B: I'm sorry. I'm going to my friend's wedding. Are you free on the first?
A: Well, I . . . .

July

Sunday	Monday	Tuesday	Wednesday	Thursday	Friday	Saturday
					1 dinner with Lynn	2
3	4 class	5	6 ←→ 7 You want to keep these dates free. Make up excuses!		8 movie with Tom	9
10	11 ←→ 12 You hope a friend calls. Make up excuses!		13 jazz club with Mike	14 theater with Jane	15	16
17 dinner with office friends	18 class	19	20 study for exam tomorrow	21 ←→ 22 You know your old friend will probably be in town! Make up excuses!		23
24 / 31	25	26 ←→ 27 You want to keep these dates free. Make up excuses!		28 dinner for Dad's birthday	29 go dancing with Ted & Sarah	30 You might have a date with an old school friend. Make up an excuse.

B *Pair work* Now work with another "Student A." Discuss the excuses "Student B" gave you. Decide which excuses were probably true and which ones were probably not true.

"Anna said that on the ninth she had to stay home and reorganize her clothes closet. That was probably not true."

interchange **15** *DO THE RIGHT THING!*

A What would you do in each of these situations? Circle **a**, **b**, or **c**. If you think you would do something else, write your suggestion next to **d**.

"What Would You Do?"

1. If an artist friend gave me a large original painting that was ugly, I would . . .
a. say something nice and put it in a closet later.
b. say that I didn't like it.
c. say thank you and hang it on the wall.
d. . . . .

2. If I saw a parent spanking a child for no reason, I would . . .
a. do nothing.
b. yell at the parent.
c. call the police.
d. . . . .

3. If I saw a student cheating on an exam, I would . . .
a. do nothing.
b. tell the teacher.
c. talk to the student about it after the exam.
d. . . . .

4. If I saw my friend's boyfriend or girlfriend with someone other than my friend, I would . . .
a. do nothing.
b. talk to my friend.
c. talk to my friend's boyfriend or girlfriend.
d. . . . .

5. If I saw a woman standing on a highway next to her car with a flat tire, I would . . .
a. do nothing.
b. stop and help her.
c. find the nearest telephone and call the police.
d. . . . .

B *Group work* Compare your choices for each situation in part A.

A: What would you do if an artist friend gave you an ugly painting?
B: Well, I would probably say that I didn't like it.
A: Really? I would . . . .

C *Class activity* Take a class survey. Find out which choice was most popular for each situation. Talk about any other suggestions people added for **d**.

interchange 16 EXCUSES, EXCUSES

Student B

A *Role play* You and your partner want to get together one evening in July. However, you are very busy and you also want to keep time open for other friends. You don't want to hurt your partner's feelings, so you make up excuses for many of the days in that month. Look at your calendar of evening plans. Then ask and answer questions to find out when you are both free. (Write your partner's excuses on the calendar.) Don't give up until you make a date.

A: Do you want to go out on the second?
B: I'm sorry. I'm going to my friend's wedding. Are you free on the first?
A: Well, I . . . .

JULY

Sunday	Monday	Tuesday	Wednesday	Thursday	Friday	Saturday
					1	2 Sue's wedding
3	4	5 movie with Bob	6	7	8	9
←— You want to keep these dates free. Make up excuses! —→				←— You don't want to make plans in case you want to get away for a few days. Make up excuses! —→		
10 visit Mom and Dad	11 office party	12	13 photography workshop at school	14	15	16
					←— Maybe an old friend will call. Make up excuses! —→	
17 visit Grandma	18	19 museum with Joe	20	21	22 party at Amy's	23 baseball game with Jim
24 family get-together / 31	25 You need a break. Make up an excuse!	26 book group meeting	27	28 need to work late tonight	29	30

B *Pair work* Now work with another "Student B." Discuss the excuses "Student A" gave you. Decide which excuses were probably true and which ones were probably not true.

"Joe said that on the sixth he had to stay home and reorganize his clothes closet. That was probably not true."

Unit Summaries

1 A TIME TO REMEMBER

KEY VOCABULARY

Nouns		Adjectives	Other	Adverbs	Prepositions
attic	memory	big	be	ago	about (yourself)
(soccer) ball	parents	favorite	begin	always	after (school)
beach	park	fine	collect	early	along (the beach)
bicycle	pet	first	follow	every (day)	at (his house)
(summer) camp	picture	fun	get up	here	from (South
cat	place	good (at . . .)	give	just	America)
chess	possession	great	go	most	in (high school)
child	rabbit	near	grow up	neither	in front of
childhood	scrapbook	OK	have (a . . . time)	not anymore	to (college)
college	shell	old	learn	now	
comic	town	scary	move	only	**Conjunctions**
dog	tree house	second	paint	originally	and
family	uncle	small	play	pretty	but
friend	vacation		Rollerblade	really	
hide-and-seek	violin	**Verbs**	spend (time)	still	**Interjections**
hobby		*Modals*	stay	there	by the way
immigrant	**Pronouns**	can	study	too	hey
job	that	could	think	very	in fact
kid	this	would	throw out		oh
lesson	yourself		walk		say
					wow

EXPRESSIONS

Greeting someone
Hi./Hello.

Introducing yourself
My name is . . ./I'm . . .
 Nice to meet you.
Good to meet you, too.

Exchanging personal information
Could you tell me (a little) about
 yourself?
 Sure. What do you want to know?
Are you from . . . ?
 Yes, I am./No, I'm not.

Where were you born?
 I was born in . . . .
Did you grow up there?
Did you go to school in . . . ?
 Yes, I did./No, I didn't.

Talking about past activities
Where did you learn to . . . ?
 Here.
How old were you when you began
to . . . ?
 I was . . . years old.
What/Where did you use to . . . ?
 When I was a kid, I used to . . . .
I used to . . . , too, when I was a kid.

Talking about past abilities
How well did you . . . ?
 I was pretty good.

Apologizing
I'm (really) sorry.

Asking for and agreeing to a favor
Can you . . . ?
 Sure.

Giving opinions
I bet . . . .

GRAMMAR EXTENSION Adverbial clauses with when

These four sentences mean the same; here, *when* means "at that time":

a) **When** I was in high school, we moved here. c) **When** we moved here, I was in high school.
b) We moved here **when** I was in high school. d) I was in high school **when** we moved here.

When an adverbial clause comes before an independent clause (as in sentences a and c), a comma is used.

2 CAUGHT IN THE RUSH

KEY VOCABULARY

Nouns
City places
airport
bank
cash machine
dance club
department store
(business) district
newsstand
restaurant
(duty-free) shop

Transportation
bicycle
 (lane/stand)
bus
 (lane/station/stop)
car
subway
 (entrance/station)
taxi
 (driver/lane/stand)
train

Other
certificate
coffee

counter
crime
cup
facility
fare
fire
government
hall
hamburger
highway
(half) hour
idea
letter
location
ma'am
(news)paper
noise
parking
 (garage/light/space)
pedestrian
police (officer)
(air) pollution
question
restroom
route
rush hour
stop (light/sign)

street (light/sign)
system
telephone
traffic
 (light/sign/jam)

Pronoun
one

Adjectives
average
cheap
close (to)
full
polite
public
special
sure
terrible
terrific
wrong

Verbs
Modal
be able to
should

Other
arrive
be allowed (to)
buy
check
come
cost
drive
feel like
find
get
improve
leave (for)
look
move
need
open
park
provide
see
take (time)
talk about
write

Adverbs
downtown
in general
much
never
quickly
right
sometimes
upstairs

Prepositions
across from
around (here)
at (rush hour)
behind
down (the hall)
except
on (the corner of)
next to

Conjunctions
however
so

Interjection
oh, no

EXPRESSIONS

Expressing a concern
There are too many . . . ./There is too much . . . .
There aren't enough . . . ./There isn't enough . . . .
We need more . . . .
There should be fewer . . . ./There should be less . . . .

Getting someone's attention
Excuse me.

Asking for and giving information
Can you tell me where . . . ?
  Let me think.
Could you tell me how often . . . ?
  Every . . . .
Do you know what time/when . . . ?
  Sorry. I don't know.
Just one more thing.
  Yes?

Asking a rhetorical question
Why is there never a . . . when you need one?
  Good question.

Thanking someone
Thanks (a lot).

Making a suggestion
Let's (go and) . . . .

Expressing probability
It should . . . .

GRAMMAR EXTENSION Word order with Wh-words

Direct question

Where	is	the bank?
Wh-word	verb	subject

Indirect question

Do you know	where	the bank	is?
	Wh-word	subject	verb

Statement

I don't know	where	the bank	is.
	Wh-word	subject	verb

3 TIME FOR A CHANGE!

KEY VOCABULARY

Nouns
Houses/Apartments
bathroom
bedroom
closet
kitchen
living room
window

Other
appearance
(rock) band
class
clothes
guitar
homework
interest
leisure
life
(a) lot (of)
money
musician
neighborhood
personality
skill

Pronouns
something
somewhere

Adjectives
*Describing houses
  and apartments*
bright
comfortable
convenient
cramped
dangerous
dark
dingy
expensive
huge
inconvenient
large
modern
new
noisy
private
quiet
reasonable
safe
shabby
spacious

Other
boring
different
difficult
easy
free
healthy
in (good) shape
last
own
part-time
single

Verbs
Modal
have to

Other
add
become
change
do (chores)
enjoy
go back
go out
like
live
make (friends)

pay
read
rent
retire
show
take (classes)
work

Adverbs
a little
actually
all (day)
else
not at all
then
well

Prepositions
around (the house)
in (the evening)

Conjunction
though

Interjections
hmm
uh

EXPRESSIONS

Asking for and giving an opinion
What do you think?
  The . . . isn't . . . enough.
  The . . . is too . . . .
  There aren't enough . . . ./There isn't enough . . . .
  It's not as . . . as . . . .
  It doesn't have as many . . . as . . . ./ It has
    just as many . . . as . . . .

Exchanging personal information
Where are you working now?
  I'm still at the . . . .
How old are you?
  (I'm) . . . .

Expressing regret about a present situation
I wish (that) I could . . . .
I wish I didn't . . . .
I wish life were easier.

Expressing sympathy and empathy
That's too bad.
I know what you mean.

Agreeing
I don't . . . either.

Expressing interest
Really?

GRAMMAR EXTENSION Evaluations

Evaluations often include an infinitive (*to* + base verb).

adjective + enough + *infinitive*
The kitchen isn't **large enough to eat in**.

too + *adjective* + *infinitive*
The kitchen is **too small to eat in**.

4 I'VE NEVER HEARD OF THAT!

KEY VOCABULARY

Nouns
Food and beverages
bagel
banana
beef
brains
bread
cake
chicken
coconut milk
curry
(scrambled) egg
eggplant
fish
frog's legs
garlic
guacamole (dip)
honey
meat
(coconut) milk
oil
onion
pasta
peanut butter
pizza
popcorn
potato

sandwich
shrimp
snails
soup
vegetable
water

Meals
breakfast
dinner
lunch

Other
appetizer
barbecue
bowl
charcoal
check
diet
dish
ingredient
kebob
lighter fluid
marinade
menu
picnic
(food) poisoning

recipe
skewer
slice
snack
sir

Adjectives
awful
barbecued
delicious
fried
interesting
strange
toasted

Verbs
Cooking methods
bake
barbecue
boil
fry
roast
steam

Other
cut into/up
decide (on)

eat
hear of
light
make (= prepare)
marinate
pour (over)
prefer
put in/on
skip
spread
take off
try
turn over

Adverbs
ever
from time to time
lately
recently
usually
yesterday
yet

Prepositions
for (20 minutes)
in (the morning)

EXPRESSIONS

Talking about food and beverages
Have you ever eaten . . . ?
   Yes, I have./No, I haven't.
It's/They're . . . !
This/It sounds . . . ./They sound . . . .
Yum!
Ugh!/Yuck!

Ordering in a restaurant
Have you decided yet?
   Yes. I'll have . . . .
And you?
   I think I'll have the . . . .

Making and declining an offer
Like to . . . ?
   No, thanks.

Describing a procedure
First, ...
Then . . . .
Next, ...
After that, ...
Finally, ...

Stating a preference
I usually like to . . . .
I prefer to . . . .

GRAMMAR EXTENSION   Two meanings of recently

In the present perfect, *recently* means "during the period of days or weeks" or "lately."

I've eaten out a lot **recently** – three times this week.

In the past tense, *recently* means "not long ago."

I **recently** ate Korean food for the first time – last week, in fact.

5 GOING PLACES

KEY VOCABULARY

Nouns

Activities
camping
fishing
hiking
mountain climbing
rafting
reading
swimming

Other
backpack
(hiking) boots
camper
cash
condominium
country
cousin
credit card
culture
expedition
father
first-aid kit
identification
lots (of)

luggage
medication
mom
overnight bag
national park
passport
plan
plenty (of)
pocket
(hotel) reservation
shorts
suitcase
temple
thing
(plane) ticket
traveler's check
trip
vaccination
visa
wallet
weather
week
windbreaker
world

Pronoun
anyone

Adjectives
alone
back
excited
exciting
foreign
pleasant
round-trip
several
warm

Verbs
Modals
had better
must
ought to
should

Other
backpack
carry
catch up on

check on
have (time off)
lie
pack
start
take (a vacation/a walk)
think (about/of)
travel
visit

Adverbs
abroad
already
around
away
lots of
maybe
nearby
probably
so

Prepositions
around (Europe)
by (yourself)
for (a few days)

EXPRESSIONS

Talking about definite plans
Have you made any plans?
    I'm going to . . . .

Talking about possible plans
What are you going to do?
    I guess/I think I'll . . . .
    I'll probably . . . .
    Maybe I'll . . . .

Asking about length of time
For how long?
How long are you going to . . . ?
How long should we . . . ?

Expressing necessity
You (don't) have to/You must/You need to . . . .

Making a suggestion
You'd better . . . .
You ought to/should/shouldn't . . . .

Making and accepting an offer
Why don't you . . . ?
    Do you mean it? I'd love to!

GRAMMAR EXTENSION Future sentences

With present continuous

The present continuous is often used with a future meaning when we are talking about things that have already been decided on and planned.

Where **are** you **going** for your vacation?
    We're **staying** home. My grandparents **are coming** for a visit.

With simple present

The simple present is often used with a future meaning when we are talking about timetables, schedules, and so on.

When **do** you **leave**?
    Our plane **takes off** at midnight, and we **arrive** in Paris at 7:00 A.M.

KEY VOCABULARY

Nouns
block
cigarette
coat
(a) couple (of)
dollar
driveway
dry cleaning
faucet
floor
garbage
groceries
lasagna
magazine
mess
music
neighbor
oven
phone
problem
program
radio
(non-smoking) section
shoe
sound

stereo
towel
toy
trash
TV
wall

Pronoun
anything

Adjectives
broke
busy
loud
thin

Verbs
Two-part verbs
clean off/up
hang up
keep down
move into
pay back
pick up
put away/out
take off/out
throw out
turn down/off/on

Other
afford
block
drive
forget
help
lend
mind
plan (to)
realize
smoke

Adverbs
across
definitely
down
next door
(all) over
quietly
soon
through
tomorrow
totally

Prepositions
in (a minute)
on (the phone)

Conjunction
if

EXPRESSIONS

Making and agreeing/objecting to a request
Please . . . .
    Sure. No problem!
    Oh, but . . . .
Can/Could you . . . ?
    I'd be glad to.
Would you please . . . ?
    OK. I'll . . . .
Would you mind . . . ?
    Sorry. I'll . . . right away.

Apologizing
I'm sorry. I didn't realize./I forgot./I'll . . . right away.

Making a promise
I'll make sure to . . . .

Expressing annoyance
Goodness!

Expressing surprise
Are you kidding?

GRAMMAR EXTENSION *Separable and inseparable two-part words*

Some two-part verbs take a direct object and can be separated.

Put away your things.
Why don't you **put** your things **away**?
    I already **put** them **away**.

Other two-part verbs can also take direct objects but can't be separated.

Help me **look for** my new Suzanne Vega CD. I want to **listen to** it.
    Suzanne Vega? I never **heard of** her.

7 WHAT'S THIS FOR?

KEY VOCABULARY

Nouns
Machines / Appliances
battery
camcorder
CD-ROM
(laptop) computer
fax (machine)
hair dryer
microwave oven
modem
(cellular) phone
robot
satellite

Other
advice
astronomy
ATM card
attendance
behavior
(household) bill
budget
(send) button
(phone/telephone) call
chat (group/room)
cold
container
criminal
document
encyclopedia

factory
(DNA) fingerprinting
heat
in-line skate
information
instructions
Internet
jet ski
(phone) line
medical school
metal
mother
motorbike
movie
number
order
(electrical) outlet
paper (= composition)
(crime) pattern
people
person
photocopy
professor
psychotherapist
report
report card
(work) schedule
sport
task
UFO

worker
World Wide Web

Pronouns
mine
ours

Adjectives
closed
extreme
fragile
latest

Verbs
access
analyze
belong
communicate
connect
create
dial
drop
exchange
expose
get on
heat
identify
make sure
perform
place

plug
press
process
recharge
remember
research
run (a machine)
save
send
spill
store
teach
unplug
use

Adverbs
away
facedown
first of all
just about
often
on-line

Prepositions
at (a medical school)
in (a factory)
on (= about)

Interjection
uh-huh

EXPRESSIONS

Making a suggestion
Why don't you . . . ?
  Maybe I will.

Describing a use or purpose
What's this for?
  It's used for . . . ./It's used to . . . .
  I can use it for . . . ./I can use it to . . . .
What are these for?
  They're used for . . . ./They're used to . . . .
  You can use them for . . . ./You can use them to . . . .

Giving and responding to advice
First of all, don't forget to . . . .
  Got it!
Then . . . . And remember to . . . .
  That's all?
Pretty much. Just make sure to . . . . And try not to . . . .
  Good advice.

GRAMMAR EXTENSION Uncompleted infinitives

Advice
Remember to recharge the batteries.

Response with completed infinitive
I won't **forget to recharge** them.

Response with uncompleted infinitive (to avoid repetition)
I won't **forget to**.

8 LET'S CELEBRATE!

KEY VOCABULARY

Nouns
Holidays, festivals, and
   celebrations
anniversary
April Fool's Day
bachelor party
birthday
bridal shower
Carnival
engagement
Halloween
May Day
Mother's Day
New Year's Eve
party
(wedding) reception
Thanksgiving
Valentine's Day
wedding

Other
bride
candy
card
champagne
costume
couple
cranberry sauce
dancing

door
dress
fireworks
flower
gift
groom
kimono
man
mask
newlywed
night
occasion
part
period
photo
present
revolution
samba
trick
turkey
woman
word

Seasons
fall
spring
summer
winter

Pronouns
each other
everyone
ones

Adjectives
beautiful
engaged
female
long
male
Western
white
young

Verbs
ask for
attend
celebrate
change (into)
date
dress up
get
   (engaged/married/
   together)
happen
have (a party)
hold
honor

invite
knock
last
love
party
receive
return
say
serve
wear

Adverb
on . . . own

Prepositions
by (saying)
during (the reception)
on (October 31st)
with (cranberry sauce)

Interjection
Trick or treat!

EXPRESSIONS

Describing holidays, festivals, and celebrations
. . . is a day/a night when . . . .
. . . is the day when . . . .
. . . is the season when . . . .
A . . . is a time when . . . .
. . . is the month when . . . .
Before . . . , ...
After . . . , ...
When . . . , ...

Asking about customs
How old are people when they . . . ?
Is there . . . ?
Where is the . . . usually held?
What happens during the . . . ?
What do . . . wear?
What type of food is served?

GRAMMAR EXTENSION   Adverbial clauses of time

In sentences with clauses beginning with *before* and *after*, there is always one action that comes before another.

Before a man gets married, his friends give him a
party. = First, his friends give him a party; then he
gets married.

After a woman gets married, she often changes her
name. = First, she gets married; then she changes
her name.

With clauses beginning with *when*, however, either one action comes before another – and *when* means
"after" – or both actions happen at the same time.

When a woman gets married, she often changes her
name. = First, she gets married; then she changes
her name.

When a woman gets married, she usually wears a white
dress. = During the time she's getting married, she
wears a white dress. (both happen at the same time)

S-9

KEY VOCABULARY

Nouns
accident
actress
automobile
building
clothing
(common) cold
cure
education
entertainment
environment
game
golf
grocery store
gym
hospital
housing
language
loan
mall
medicine
office
population
request
shopping
sleep
space
store

sugar
supermarket
technology

Adjectives
awake
energetic
hard
high-rise
hungry
jealous
relaxed
serious
successful

Verbs
Modals
may
might

Other
fall (in love)
fit (into)
gain (weight)
give up
go on (a diet)
grow
inherit

join
miss
lose (touch/weight)
own
quit
sell
shop
star
take care of
tear down

Adverbs
even
fast
nowadays
sometime
these days
today

Prepositions
at (stores)
by (computer)
in (the next 100 years/the future)
on (TV)

Conjunction
without

EXPRESSIONS

Talking about the past
In the past, ...
People used to . . . .
. . . years ago, people . . . .

Talking about the present
These days, ...
Today, people . . . .
Nowadays, people . . . .

Talking about the future
Soon, there will be . . . .
In . . . years, people might/may . . . .
In the future, people are going to . . . .

Describing situations and possible consequences
If I . . . , I might . . . .
If you . . . , you won't be able to . . . .
If they don't . . . , they'll have to . . . .
If you . . . , you may be able to . . . .

GRAMMAR EXTENSION *Conditional sentences with* if *clauses*

In a conditional sentence about a possible situation, the simple present is usually used in the *if* clause.

If you **quit** smoking, you'll feel better.

Sometimes, however, the future with *will* is used in the *if* clause – especially if there is an offer in the consequence clause.

If you**'ll quit** smoking, I'll buy you a new car.
If you**'ll buy** me a car, I'll quit smoking.

10 *I DON'T LIKE WORKING ON WEEKENDS!*

KEY VOCABULARY

Nouns
Jobs / Occupations
accountant
architect
bookkeeper
doctor
executive
flight attendant
journalist
lawyer
marine biologist
model
novelist
nurse
songwriter
stockbroker
teacher
waiter
writer

Other
bookstore
boss
co-worker
deadline
decision
diploma
driver's license
experience
math
meeting
mistake
sales
semester
stuff
team

Adjectives
Personality traits
bad-tempered
creative
critical
disorganized
efficient
forgetful
generous
hard-working
impatient
level-headed
moody
patient
punctual
reliable
shy
strict
unfriendly

Other
retail

Verbs
be interested (in)
commute
file
make (a decision/a mistake)
meet (a deadline)
organize
solve
stand

Prepositions
during (the week)
from (nine to five)
in (sales)
on (weekends)

Interjections
Let's see.
Mmm.

EXPRESSIONS

**Expressing and agreeing
with feelings and opinions**
I like/hate enjoy . . . .
  So do I.
I'm interested in . . . ./
I'm good at . . . .
  So am I.
I'm not good at . . . .
  Neither am I.
I don't mind . . . .
  Neither do I.
I can't stand . . . .
  Neither can I.

**Expressing and disagreeing
with feelings and opinions**
I like/enjoy . . . .
  Oh, I don't.
I hate . . . .
  Really? I like . . . .
I'm interested in . . . ./
I'm good at . . . .
  Gee, I'm not.
I'm not good at . . . .
  I am!
I can't stand . . . .
  Oh, I don't mind.

**Talking about possible
occupations**
I'd make a good/bad . . . because . . .
  I'm . . . and I like/don't like . . . .
I wouldn't want to be a/an . . .
  because I'm too . . . .
I could (never) be a/an . . .
  because I'm not good at . . . .
I wouldn't mind working as a/an . . .
  because I really like . . . .

GRAMMAR EXTENSION *Verbs followed by either a gerund or an infinitive*

You can use either a gerund (verb + *-ing*) or an infinitive (*to* + verb) after these verbs – without changing the meaning of the sentence:

like   love   hate   can't stand   begin/start   continue

I like **commuting/to commute** to work.
I love **meeting/to meet** new people.
I hate **writing/to write** reports.
I can't stand **sitting/to sit** in meetings.
I've **begun/started looking for/to look for** a new job.
We continue **having/to have** problems with our boss.

IT'S REALLY WORTH SEEING!

KEY VOCABULARY

Nouns			Verbs	
Currencies	harbor	tomb	accept	sightsee
baht	industry	tourism	approach	speak
dollar	light bulb	travel agent	build	welcome
peso	mining	visitor	compose	
pound	monument	wheat	design	**Adverbs**
yen	novel	wife	develop	a great deal (of)
	opera		direct	around
	painting	**Pronoun**	discover	inside
Other	phonograph	which	get to	
advance	prime minister		govern	**Prepositions**
album	prince	**Adjectives**	invent	on (the left/the right)
(cartoon) character	product	agricultural	locate	since (1886)
cheese	radium	both	make up	to (the top)
crown	religion	digital	manufacture	
electronics	sculptor	federal	perform	**Interjection**
elevator	stair	incredible	produce	of course
engineering	state	religious	record	
film	statue			
hair salon	step			

EXPRESSIONS

Expressing amazement
Wow!
Incredible, isn't it?

**Describing works of art,
inventions, and discoveries**
. . . was built/composed/created/
   designed/directed/painted/
   recorded/written by . . . .
. . . was developed/discovered/
   invented/produced by. . . .

Asking about a country
Where is . . . located?
What languages are spoken in . . . ?
What currency is used in . . . ?
Is English spoken (much) there?
Are credit cards accepted there?

Responding to difficult questions
I'm not sure. Isn't it . . . ?
I think . . . , but I'm not sure.
I really have no idea.
How would I know?

Expressing confusion
Huh?
What?
Where?

GRAMMAR EXTENSION · *Subject–verb agreement in passive sentences*

With expressions of quantity with of

> The form of *be* – singular or plural – is determined by the noun or pronoun that follows *of*.

A lot of coffee **is** grown in Brazil.
A great deal of it **is** sent to other countries.

A lot of agricultural products **are** grown in Brazil.
Some of them **are** sold at local markets.

With singular nouns ending in -s

> The singular form of *be* is used.

The Philippines **is** made up of more than 7,000 islands.
The news that**'s** printed in many papers is incredible.
Mathematics **is** taught to very young children.

With plural nouns not ending in -s

> The plural form of *be* is used.

The police **were** called after the accident.
People **are** often helped by their neighbors.

12 IT'S BEEN A LONG TIME!

KEY VOCABULARY

Nouns
Human ages
adolescent
(young) adult
baby
boy
elderly person
girl
infant
middle-aged person
teenager

Other
arm
audition
break
customer
drama school
exercise
fat
graduate school
grandfather
grandmother
grandparent
journalism
power
seafood
suburbs
tutor

Adjectives
lucky
tiny

Verbs
break
enter
finish
get into
go out
ice-skate
offer
ring
run out (of)
save up

Adverbs
almost
full time
last
luckily
out of

Prepositions
as (a waitress)
between (the ages of 1 and 12)
for (the last six months)
in (ages)
within (a few weeks)

Conjunction
while

EXPRESSIONS

Greeting someone after a long time
I haven't seen you in ages.
Has it been . . . since I last saw you?

Talking about past events
I was . . . , but I never . . . .
I was . . . , when I . . . .
While I was . . . , ...

Exchanging personal information
Have you been doing anything exciting recently?
   Yes, I have./No, I haven't.
What have you been doing lately/ these days?
   I've been . . . .
How long have you been doing that?
   For . . . .
How have you been?
   Great!

Expressing interest and surprise
Wow, what a lucky break!
Wow! That's incredible!
Wow! Tell me more.
Oh, really? That's interesting.
Really? I didn't know that!
Oh, I see.
Gee, I had no idea.

Asking for a reason
How come?

GRAMMAR EXTENSION during *and* while

during + *noun*
Someone called **during** dinner.

while + *subject* + *verb*
Someone called **while** we were having dinner.

13 A TERRIFIC BOOK, BUT A TERRIBLE MOVIE!

KEY VOCABULARY

Nouns
Movies
action movie
comedy
horror movie
musical
mystery
nature film
romance
western

Other
actor
alien
composer
critic
detective show
director
event
guy
law firm
planet
rating
review
scene
script

secret agent
song
special effect
star
studio
video

Adjectives
absurd
amazing
another
bizarre
brave
corrupt
disgusting
dreadful
dumb
fabulous
fascinating
frightening
horrible
marvelous
main
odd
outstanding
ridiculous

silly
stupid
surprising
unusual
weird
wonderful

Verbs
amaze
bore
end
fascinate
chase (after)
put down
star
surprise
take place

Adverbs
again
kind of

Preposition
of (all time)

EXPRESSIONS

Giving opinions about movies, books, and people
I'm interested in . . . .
   Now that sounds good.
I thought . . . was an exciting book.
I'm fascinated by . . . .
I think . . . is a very interesting actor.
I find . . . fascinating.

Describing movies, books, and people
It's the movie which/that . . . .
It was a great book which/that . . . .
It's about a man/woman who/that . . . .
He's/She's . . . that . . . .

Reminding someone
You know . . . .

GRAMMAR EXTENSION   Prepositions used with past participles

Some past participles used as adjectives can be followed by a preposition + noun/gerund. Here are some examples:

amazed at
bored with/by
confused by
embarrassed by

disappointed by/in/with
disgusted with/by
fascinated with/by
frightened of/at

interested in
scared of
surprised at/by
tired of

People are often **amazed at** the special effects in movies these days.
I was very **disappointed in** Tom Cruise's last movie; I was **surprised at** how silly it was.
We're **tired of** seeing the same actors over and over.

14 SO THAT'S WHAT IT MEANS!

KEY VOCABULARY

Nouns
bridge
cloud
falsehood
gesture
gift shop
hard hat
head
lane
lining
mountain
museum
path
peace
penny
poison
proverb
road sign
seat belt

silver
stitch
truth

Adjectives
angry
annoyed/annoying
careful
confused/confusing
crazy
embarrassed/
   embarrassing
false
perfect
recyclable
scared
shocked/shocking
tired
true

Verbs
Modals
can
could
have (got) to
may
might
must

Other
agree (with)
burn
earn
fasten
go away
hatch
litter
notice
pass
remove

seem
state
touch
turn
wait
win
wonder

Adverbs
not exactly
perhaps
slow

Prepositions
from (side to side)
in (time)
off (the path)
on (one side/the other)

EXPRESSIONS

Hypothesizing
It might/may mean . . . .
It could mean . . . .
Maybe/Perhaps it means . . . .

Making a logical assumption
That must mean . . . .
That probably means . . . .

Expressing permission
You can . . . .
You're allowed to . . . .

Expressing prohibition
You can't . . . .
You're not allowed to . . . .

Expressing obligation
You have to . . . .
You've got to . . . .

Disagreeing
I don't think so.

GRAMMAR EXTENSION   Modals to express different degrees of certainty

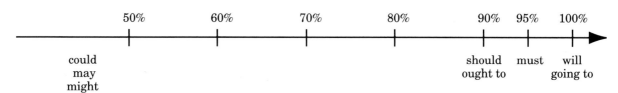

I wonder where this road goes.
   It could/may/might go . . . . = The speaker has no information and is only guessing.
   It should/ought to go . . . . = The speaker has some information.
   It must go . . . . = The speaker is almost sure.
   It will go . . . . = The speaker is sure.

S-15

WHAT WOULD YOU DO?

KEY VOCABULARY

Nouns
aunt
burglar
caller
casino
cigarette lighter
classmate
comb
counselor
drinking problem
exam
father-in-law
girlfriend
houseguest
jail
jewelry
lottery
luck
note
opportunity
owner
parking lot
radio talk show
regret
salesclerk
set (of keys)
way

Pronouns
anybody
someone

Adjectives
bad
else
honest
messy
valuable

Verbs
Modals
could
might
would

Other
admit
borrow
cheat
come back
deny
disagree
dislike
divorce
double

fight
get rid of
give back
invest
lie
lock (out)
marry
refuse
shoplift
steal
swim
thank
warn

Adverbs
overseas
straight

Prepositions
by (mistake)
for (myself)
on (a test/the street)

Conjunction
as

EXPRESSIONS

Describing imaginary situations and consequences in the present
What would you do if . . . ?
  If I . . . , I'd/I wouldn't/I might/I could . . . .

Talking about imaginary or hypothetical actions in the past
What would you have done?
  I would have . . . .
  I wouldn't have done anything.
What should I have done?
  You should have . . . .
  You shouldn't have . . . .

Emphatically saying no
No way!

Saying someone is right
Hmm. You've got a point there.

Expressing gladness/relief
Thank goodness!

GRAMMAR EXTENSION Past modals

Use *could have* or *might have* + past participle to say there was an opportunity for something to have happened although it didn't happen.

You **could have/might have waited** a little longer. = You had the chance and it was possible to wait a little longer – but you didn't wait.

KEY VOCABULARY

Nouns
anger
answering machine
apology
appointment
baseball bat
bathing suit
belly dancing
CD
complaint
compliment
concern
congratulations
criticism
excuse
flu
hairdresser
invitation
joke
lie
message
psychic

reason
roommate
soda
sympathy
truth
wrestling match

Verbs
bring
express
fly (in)
have (the flu)
let (in)
make (a date/plans)
pick up (someone)
promise
wait for

Adverb
out of (town)

EXPRESSIONS

Exchanging personal information
How are things?
   Just fine, thanks.
What's up?
   Well, I . . . .

Talking on the phone
Hi, ... This is . . . .
   Oh, hi.

Reporting requests
. . . asked/told me to . . . .
. . . said to . . . .
. . . asked/told me not to . . . .
. . . said not to . . . .

Reported statements
. . . said (that) . . . .
. . . told me (that) . . . .

Expressing regret
That's too bad.
I'm really sorry.
   I'm sorry, too.

Saying you remember
Oh, that's right!

GRAMMAR EXTENSION *Reported speech*

It is not always necessary to change the verb in reported speech:

- if you're reporting something that you feel is still true:

Mark said, "I need a vacation."
  = Mark said he **needs** (*or* **needed**) a vacation.

- if you're reporting something soon after it was said:

Dr. Jones just said, "I'm ready for my next appointment."
  = Dr. Jones said she **is** (or **was**) ready for her next appointment.

- if the verb is in the simple past:

Don said, "I made a date with Jill."
  = Don said he **made** (*or* **had made**) a date with Jill.

Appendix

COUNTRIES AND NATIONALITIES

This is a partial list of countries, many
of which are presented in this book.

Argentina	Argentine	Germany	German	the Philippines	Filipino
Australia	Australian	Greece	Greek	Poland	Polish
Austria	Austrian	Hungary	Hungarian	Russia	Russian
Brazil	Brazilian	India	Indian	Singapore	Singaporean
Bolivia	Bolivian	Indonesia	Indonesian	Spain	Spanish
Canada	Canadian	Ireland	Irish	Switzerland	Swiss
Chile	Chilean	Italy	Italian	Thailand	Thai
China	Chinese	Japan	Japanese	Turkey	Turkish
Colombia	Colombian	Korea	Korean	Peru	Peruvian
Costa Rica	Costa Rican	Lebanon	Lebanese	the United Kingdom	British
Ecuador	Ecuadorian	Malaysia	Malaysian	the United States	American
Egypt	Egyptian	Mexico	Mexican	Uruguay	Uruguayan
England	English	Morocco	Moroccan		
France	French	New Zealand	New Zealander		

NUMBERS

0	1	2	3	4	5	6	7	8
zero	one	two	three	four	five	six	seven	eight

9	10	11	12	13	14	15	16	17
nine	ten	eleven	twelve	thirteen	fourteen	fifteen	sixteen	seventeen

18	19	20	21	22	30	40	50	60
eighteen	nineteen	twenty	twenty-one	twenty-two	thirty	forty	fifty	sixty

70	80	90	100	1,000
seventy	eighty	ninety	one hundred (a hundred)	one thousand (a thousand)

COMPARATIVE AND SUPERLATIVE ADJECTIVES

1. Adjective with -er and -est

big	dirty	high	old	tall
busy	dry	hot	pretty	ugly
cheap	easy	large	quiet	warm
clean	fast	light	safe	wet
close	friendly	long	scary	young
cold	funny	mild	short	
cool	great	new	slow	
deep	heavy	nice	small	

2. Adjectives with *more* and *most*

attractive	exciting	outgoing
beautiful	expensive	popular
boring	famous	relaxing
crowded	important	stressful
dangerous	interesting	difficult
delicious		

3. Irregular adjectives

good → better → best
bad → worse → the worst

PRONUNCIATION OF REGULAR PAST FORMS

with /d/	*with* /t/	*with* /ɪd/
studied	worked	invited
stayed	watched	visited

IRREGULAR VERBS

Present	Past	Participle	Present	Past	Participle
(be) am/is, are	was, were	been	make	made	made
become	became	become	meet	met	met
break	broke	broken	pay	paid	paid
bring	brought	brought	put	put	put
build	built	built	quit	quit	quit
buy	bought	bought	read	read	read
come	came	come	ride	rode	ridden
cost	cost	cost	ring	rang	rung
cut	cut	cut	run	ran	run
do	did	done	say	said	said
drink	drank	drunk	see	saw	seen
drive	drove	driven	sell	sold	sold
eat	ate	eaten	send	sent	sent
fall	fell	fallen	set	set	set
feel	felt	felt	sit	sat	sat
fight	fought	fought	sleep	slept	slept
find	found	found	speak	spoke	spoken
fly	flew	flown	spend	spent	spent
forget	forgot	forgotten	stand	stood	stood
get	got	gotten	steal	stole	stolen
give	gave	given	swim	swam	swum
go	went	gone	take	took	taken
grow	grew	grown	teach	taught	taught
have	had	had	tell	told	told
hear	heard	heard	think	thought	thought
hold	held	held	wear	wore	worn
keep	kept	kept	win	won	won
lend	lent	lent	write	wrote	written
lose	lost	lost			

ANSWER KEY   Unit 11, Exercise 10, page 70

1. in South America
2. English, Malay, Chinese, and Tamil
3. Canada, China, France, India, Russia, U.S.
4. Burma, India, Kenya, Malaysia, Nigeria, Pakistan, the Philippines, Singapore, Sri Lanka, Sudan, Tanzania, among other countries
5. Belgium, Canada, France, Haiti, Luxembourg, Morocco, Senegal, Switzerland, Tunisia, among other countries
6. Australia, Canada, Denmark, Italy, Great Britain, Japan, Malaysia, the Netherlands, Norway, Portugal, Spain, Sweden, among other countries

Acknowledgments

ILLUSTRATIONS

Jack and Judith DeGaffenried
89 *(bottom)*
Randy Jones 2, 3, 8, 14, 29, 34 38, 43, 45, 58, 63 *(top)*, 66, 75 *(bottom)*, 76, 78, 79, 86 *(top)*, 87, 91, 93, 98, 100, 101, IC-2, IC-3, IC-7, IC-9 *(top)*, IC-10 *(top)*, IC-15, IC-18, IC-20
Susann Jones IC-20
Mark Kaufman 14, 15, 22, 23, 31 *(top)*, 35, 36 *(bottom)*, 44, 49, 75 *(top)*, 86 *(bottom)*, 92, 99
Kevin Spaulding 5, 28, 34 *(bottom)*, 40, 52, 54 *(top)*, 57, 63 *(bottom)*, 89, 94
Bill Thomson 69, 95
Sam Viviano 6, 11, 17, 18, 20, 27, 31 *(bottom)*, 36 *(top)*, 37, 47, 52 *(top)*, 53, 54 *(bottom)*, 56, 60, 72, 73, 84, 88, 96, 102, 103, 104, IC-4, IC-5, IC-9 *(bottom)*, IC-10 *(bottom)*, IC-12, IC-13, IC-14, IC-17

PHOTOGRAPHIC CREDITS

The authors and publishers are grateful for permission to reproduce the following photographs. Every endeavor has been made to contact copyright owners, and apologies are expressed for omissions.

2 © Remi Benali/Gamma Liaison

5 *(left)* © Mug Shots/The Stock Market; *(right)* © Ariel Skelley/The Stock Market

6 © Tony Freeman/PhotoEdit

7 *(left)* © Globe Photos; *(right)* © Barry King/Gamma Liaison

8 *(left)* © Patti McConville/The Image Bank; *(right)* © Grant V. Faint/The Image Bank

9 © Dick Luria/FPG International

12 © Michael Yamashita/Gamma Liaison

13 *(left to right)* © Jeff Greenberg/Omni Photo Communications; courtesy of Netherlands Board of Tourism; © Hugo de Vries, courtesy of State of Hawaii Department of Transportation

19 *(left)* PEOPLE Weekly © 1996 Ed Lallo; *(right)* © Mel Neale

20 (feijoada) © Paulo Fridman/International Stock; (mee krob and won ton soup) From *Sunset Oriental Cookbook*, © 1970, Sunset Books Inc., Menlo Park, CA; (ceviche) © Peter Johansky/Envision

21 © Bill Bachmann/PhotoEdit

24 *(left to right)* © Joel Glenn/The Image Bank; © Ed Bock/The Stock Market; © David Jeffrey/The Image Bank; © Roy Morsch/The Stock Market

25 © Steven Needham/Envision

26 *(both)* © SuperStock

27 © Le Goy/Gamma Liaison

30 © David Ball/Tony Stone Images

32 © Telegraph Colour Library/FPG International

33 *(top)* © Alan Becker/The Image Bank; *(bottom)* © German Youth Hostel Assoc./HI-AYH

39 *(left)* © Beth Whitman, courtesy of The Fresh Air Fund; *(right)* © Jeffrey Sylvester/FPG International

41 *(top to bottom)* © G.S.O. Images/The Image Bank; © David Ash/Tony Stone Images; © Garry Gay/The Image Bank

42 *(left to right)* © Richard Nowitz/FPG International; © Zigy Kaluzny/Tony Stone Images; © Flip Chalfant/The Image Bank

43 (microwave and hair dryer) courtesy of Sears, Roebuck and Co.; (laptop computer) courtesy of IBM Corporation

44 *(top row, left to right)* courtesy of Sears, Roebuck and Co.; courtesy of Yamaha Motor Corporation, U.S.A.; courtesy of Sears, Roebuck and Co.; *(bottom row, left to right)* courtesy of Rollerblade, Inc.; courtesy of The Long Island Savings Bank; courtesy of Kawasaki Motors Corp., U.S.A.

48 *(top to bottom)* © Ary Diesendruck/Tony Stone Images; © Martha Cooper/Viesti Associates; © Robert Frerck/Tony Stone Images; © Ron Behrmann Photography/International Stock

49 © Satoru Ohmori/Gamma Liaison

50 *(clockwise from top right)* © Paul Chesley/Tony Stone Images; © Josef Beck/FPG International; © Spencer Grant/Gamma Liaison

51 *(left to right)* © Robert Frerck/Odyssey Productions/Chicago; courtesy of Korean Cultural Service; © AP/Wide World Photos

52 © Thomas Zimmermann/FPG International

54 *(left)* © Culver Collection/SuperStock; *(right)* © Etienne de Malglaive/Gamma Liaison

55 © Michael Newman/PhotoEdit

56 © SuperStock

59 © Ed Taylor Studio/FPG International

61 © Paul Chesley/Tony Stone Images

62 *(left to right)* © Terry Qing/FPG International; © Tom Rosenthal/SuperStock; © Jeffrey Zaruba/Tony Stone Images

64 © David Young-Wolff/PhotoEdit

65 © Stewart Cohen/Tony Stone Images

67 *(Mona Lisa)* © Musee du Louvre, Paris/Giraudon, Paris/SuperStock; *(La Bohème)* © Photofest; *(To Kill a Mockingbird)* reprinted by permission of Warner Books, Inc.; *(E.T.)* © Universal/The Kobal Collection; *(Thriller)* © Dick Zimmerman, reprinted by permission of Epic Records

68 *(left to right)* © Fergus O'Brien/FPG International; © Dennis Hallinan/FPG International; © Bob Higbee/FPG International

70 *(top)* © Jean Claude Francolon/Gamma Liaison; *(bottom)* © Robert Frerck/Tony Stone Images

71 *(top to bottom)* © Guy Marche/FPG International; © David Louis Olson/National Geographic Society; © Gail Shumway/FPG International

72 *(left)* © Evan Agostini/Gamma Liaison; *(right)* © Andrea Renault/Globe Photos

74 © Arthur Tilley/FPG International

77 *(top to bottom)* © Keith Bernstein/FSP/Gamma Liaison; © Mobile Press Register/Gamma Liaison; © J.L. Bulcao/Gamma Liaison

78 © Emmanuel Faure/SuperStock

79 *(left)* © Tony Stone Images; *(right)* © Roberto Arakaki/International Stock

80 © Benainous/Duclos/Gamma Liaison

81 *(top)* © Globe Photos; *(bottom)* © Brad Markel/Gamma Liaison

83 *(top to bottom)* © Globe Photos; © United Artists/The Kobal Collection; © MGM/The Kobal Collection

85 © Lucas Film/20th Century Fox/The Kobal Collection

97 © SuperStock

105 *(top)* © Universal/The Kobal Collection; *(bottom)* © Tom Stewart/The Stock Market

IC-6 *(top)* © Ken Gallard/International Stock; *(bottom)* © John Michael/International Stock

IC-8 *(top)* © Lorentz Gullachsen/Tony Stone Images; *(bottom)* © Robert Brown Photography/International Stock

IC-11 *(left to right)* © Jon Riley/Tony Stone Images; © Rob Lewine/The Stock Market; © John Pinderhughes/The Stock Market